BRITISH DESIGN *image & identity*

BRITISH DESIGN
image & identity

frederique huygen

THAMES AND HUDSON

IN ASSOCIATION WITH

MUSEUM BOYMANS-VAN BEUNINGEN

First published in Great Britain by Thames and Hudson Ltd, London.
© 1989 Museum Boymans-van Beuningen/Frederique Huygen.

Printed and bound in the Netherlands by Lecturis bv.
Designed by Cara Gallardo and Richard Smith at Peter Saville Associates.
Translated by John Kirkpatrick.

CONTENTS

Acknowledgments

The year in which I wrote this book, 1988, has been proclaimed the year of William and Mary, and commemorates the bonds between the Netherlands and Great Britain. This book is a by-product of that tercentenary, as it appears on the occasion of the exhibition on British design in the Boymans Museum in Rotterdam, itself partly prompted by the commemoration. My initial thanks, then, must go to Julian Andrews, Director of the British Council in Amsterdam, who was the first to draw attention to the link between William and Mary and industrial design.

Although this link is not directly discernible at first sight, the bonds in this area between the two countries are on further inspection very closely-knit indeed. Dutch writers and early socialists were greatly inspired by the ideas of William Morris. His lectures were translated early on in the Netherlands, and in 1903 published in bookform. In the fields of jewellery, ceramics, and graphic design the exchange between the two countries, especially in recent decades, has been very intense. Moreover, many Dutch designers have lived and worked in Britain, and many still do.

Although this book is not specially concerned with these mutual influences, it is in itself a product of connections between the two countries. For it is only due to the effort and enthusiasm of many British and Dutch people that this book is now before you. So I am greatly indebted to all those who in one way or another have helped put it there. I would here like to mention in particular Deyan Sudjic, editor of the magazine *Blueprint*, as the person who stimulated me into writing this book in the first place. His intelligent comments and information helped to make it what it is. Profuse thanks are due also to Peter Dormer and John Thackara of Design Analysis International for all the support they have given me; not only by way of their knowledge, insight, and information, but also in the inspiring talks we had. My thanks, too, go to Saskia de Bodt, Thames & Hudson and Edi Cohen for their criticism and encouragement.

I would also like to express my unbounded appreciation of all those who collaborated with me on this book, from designer to printer; in particular Anne Marie Ehrlich, Cara Gallardo, Jan Jongepier, John Kirkpatrick, Peter Saville, Ineke Tirion-Beijerinck, Bert Vreeken, Brett Wickins, and Hester Wolters. To the photographer Ian Dobbie I am particularly indebted for the sheer energy and dedication with which he has rendered in visual terms the image and identity of British design. Everyone who helped him achieve this, in particular Angela Gusty, has my gratitude too. Peter van Gorssel is another who with his advice has contributed much to this book. Further, I would like to thank all those who gave up their time to speak to me and to share thoughts with me on the British identity in design: Ron Arad, Glenda Bailey, Lewis Blackwell, Brian Boylan, Floris van den Broecke, Janet Burney, Dinah Casson, Anton Corbijn, Mike Dempsey, Gert Dumbar, James Dyson, Malcolm Garrett, Kaspar de Graaf, Kenneth Grange, Laurence Gunzi, Rune Gustafson, Brian Johnson, Robin Kinross, Roger Mann, Catherine McDermott, Alex McDowell, Valerie Mendes, Suzy Menkes, Dick Seymour, Nigel Stone, Carlos Virgile, Daniel Weil, and Peter York.

Last, but by no means least, I would like to thank my family and friends, and the inventors of the computer programme Wordperfect.

Preface

The title *British Design, Image and Identity* immediately brings us face to face with an intricate linguistic problem concerning the adjectives *English* and *British*. For a foreigner the country will always be England, L'Angleterre, Engeland, L'Inghilterra; a reminder of the time when England ruled the group of islands to the west of the European mainland. The United Kingdom (including Northern Ireland) and Great Britain (without it) – terms formally more correct, but to Dutch ears having a more pompous ring – are here used only by those familiar with their British significance.

Also foreigners experience the differences in nuance between *British* and *English* in a way quite unlike that of the British themselves. Thus before embarking on this book, the word British brought to my mind descriptions like Empire, India, citizen, courteous, formal, superior, arrogant; whereas the adjective English had more of rolling hills, literature, roses, country estates, *Brideshead Revisited*, Oxford, and Saville Row suits. In the United Kingdom itself, according to Tom Nairn in his book *The Enchanted Glass: Britain and its Monarchy* of 1988, Great Britain stands for imperial robes, and Britain for the boring lounge suit; England is poetic but troublesome and the British

Isles too geographical. A ticklish problem indeed. One could say, for instance, that Englishness is a more accurate description, as British culture seems to be dictated by the English. One may indeed wonder if such a thing as Britishness exists at all, as historically speaking the United Kingdom is made up of components (England, Scotland, Wales, Northern Ireland) each with very much its own identity. While some elements of this individuality have been absorbed in a greater whole, other continue to exist in their own right. Is Great Britain really one nation? As the question of whether there is a British national culture is not mine to answer – nor is it the subject of this book – I have opted for the geographical definition and use either Britain or the United Kingdom; if only because many of the developments, persons, and events described here are from beyond England's borders. This also explains my use of the – to my mind – more neutral terms British and Britishness.

The word *design* signifies so many different things: a process, a means of promoting sales, and a stage on the road to production. It enhances products, and sells them; it solves problems and conveys ideas; it is artistic and commercial, intellectual and physical. This many-sidedness – or ambiguity – is something we have to learn to live with, as a historically incontravertible fact. Where it would not otherwise be obvious from the context as to which aspect was being discussed, my wording has been more specific. Whenever the word design appears in inverted commas, I am referring to the polluted meaning of the word, its use as a prefix for sales purposes, as 'added value', as a symbol of status and supposed quality, because these days anything and everything is labelled design.

British Design, Image and Identity sets out to examine the question of what makes designing in Britain stand out. Just what is it that makes British design so different, so appealing? How, and why, does it differ from that of other countries? Why are some of its aspects more developed than others? Being an enquiry into differences makes it just as much an investigation of similarities. Are there particular characteristics common to British design, and if so, which socio-cultural backgrounds can claim them? An investigation into the British identity in design comes naturally enough to a non-Briton like myself; fired by curiosity into searching for those special ingredients, and, along the way, acquiring a fascination for this paradoxical, many-layered culture with its marvellous language. Being an outsider brings with it the obvious advantages and disadvantages. I can only hope that being in this position has helped to present an interesting view of design in Britain, for that, after all, is what this book sets out to achieve.

But my line of inquiry was motivated also by the vast amount of existing literature on design. The deluge of superficial coffee table books we have been subjected to during recent years has contributed to a gratifying surge of interest in the subject. At the same time, it denotes the end of a period, and so this relatively new field now lies fallow for new and more thorough cultivation. The cataloguing, summing up, and descriptions, however useful, will, in my opinion, have to make way for a more interpretative approach. My interest in any case is far more in framing questions and bringing up problems than in attempting a comprehensive study.

In addition, I have been much inspired by history books, to me so stimulating because they are continually drawing new conclusions on the basis of existing facts. Each subject sets off a concatenation of actions and reactions. The hypothesis of one author is immediately given a new interpretation by another. And this, surely, is what the writing of history is all about. Are not interpretations the crux of the matter, the thing that makes it exciting, rather than plain facts? And can a book be much more than that anyway? An interpretation; a train of thought; an argument; a point of view based on existing things which creates the next link in the chain?

Frederique Huygen
Rotterdam, November 1988

INTRODUCTION

British design: Burberry raincoats, floral interior fabrics, Jaguars, Shetland pullovers, Dunhill lighters, and Wedgwood pottery. Tradition, respectability, and quality. This sort of Britishness forms but a part of this book, for there are many more faces to British design than the clichés listed above.

Of this the developments of the last fifteen years are conclusive proof. Britain's retail trade was converted en masse to modern design; design consultancies swelled both in number and in scope; British fashion suddenly came back with a vengeance to the international limelight; craft enjoyed a revival; young British designers overran the media, and livened things up again with their way-out furniture; new magazines signalled new tendencies in graphic design; and media-orientated fields such as television, pop videos, music, and advertising provided new areas for designers to explore.

Recent changes like these put British design history as we know it in quite another light. In most literature on the subject it all began with Sir Robert Peel who in 1832 questioned the standard of British design in a parliamentary debate. The results were the founding of the first museum of applied arts and the Great Exhibition of 1851 in the Crystal Palace. British design history then continues by way of the Arts and Crafts movement to the modern outlook of the DIA (Design and Industries Association) and the CoID (Council of Industrial Design). Seen as milestones of the postwar period are the exhibition Britain Can Make It (1946) and the Festival of Britain (1951), national events which gave interest in, and the acceptance of, design a push in the right direction. Then, after further professionalisation, design came to maturity during the fifties, sixties, and seventies. Do the revolutionary developments of the eighties occupy a position outside this evolutionary process or can we discern some sort of continuity in it? This is one of the questions raised by the subject of this book. However, unlike the picture history gives us, *British Design, Image and Identity* is no linear, progressive history, but rather a thematic one.

The book's point of departure is shaped on one hand by these recent phenomena, which I will attempt to put in a specific context. (This context is not only formed by economic, social, and other societal issues, but – especially in a country so dominated by tradition – is also rooted in the historical developments which led to them.) On the other hand, it is shaped by characteristics long part of British design, such as the craft tradition, the heavily social and moral slant that began with Morris, and a practical, down-to-earth approach.

The book gets underway with a general character study of British design, which to me has an unmistakable air of moderation and commonsense. With what culturally determined conditions could this property be linked? Paradoxically enough, British design does include some quite definite extremes, from pageantry to punk. To what, then, are these related?

Chapter two, England as the Garden, looks at the continuation of tradition and rural values, so crucial for the crafts, and thus for later design, in Britain. During recent years, however, this metaphor has been paired with the idea of an anti-industrial culture. The inestimably important craft tradition which began with Morris was even rooted in the rejection of a capitalist, industrial society. What sort of foundations did this lay for Britain's industrial design?

Against this, in chapter three, I have set the tradition of inventors and entrepreneurs, who in previous centuries turned the land of the Industrial Revolution into The Workshop of the World. What has become of this tradition in the twentieth century, and what interactions are there between economics, industry, and designing?

Forming a stark contrast to the craft-based past – and in the light of the hardly exciting, almost static postwar design history – is the wellnigh revolutionary upsurge of the giant design consultancies of the eighties. No other country can boast such an explosive growth. No longer is design a fringe phenomenon as it was in the fifties; it has become 'big business'. Chapter four takes a look at these consultancies and their activities, and attempts to account for their rapid ascent.

Another remarkable and recent phenomenon, tied in with the rise of the design consultancies, is the 'design' retail boom. The British High Street has in a matter of years been transformed into a super-seductive shoppers' paradise, a heaven on earth for the pampered consumer. Splendidly turned out boutiques vie for the custom of the status-conscious 'yuppie' by way of distinctive and meticulously designed interiors. New shopping chains, each trying to outdo the other, are sprouting up everywhere. Their museumlike interiors together with the clothes and accessories on sale and the packaging, achieve a perfect 'total design'. Chapter five endeavours

to ascertain why it is that London calls the tune in this field, and whether there are parallels here with the sixties.

Chapters six and seven enter into the underlying values that have long governed British design, beginning with the emphasis on social aspects which in the eighties are threatened with being snowed under by commercial values embodied by the giant consultancies. Firstly, I shall be looking at the government and design in the public sector; secondly, I shall be trying to find out what became of the social consciousness first advanced by British designers like Morris and Ruskin.

Chapter seven concentrates on the pragmatism I consider to be another specific property of British design. Values like usefulness and 'fitness for purpose' have always been heavily stressed in British design, the practical side often coming before intellectual theory and exuberant fantasy. Extreme trends in British design are few and far between. How did British designers react to radical movements from abroad, such as the Modern Movement or Memphis? Is British design an insular affair, or does it effortlessly absorb influences from abroad?

Chapter eight follows on from the pragmatism of 'doing-as-designing' in chapter seven, and focuses on individualism and craftwork. It seems that from the design ranks there has emerged a self-willed, wayward generation of designers displaying a high level of creative individuality. More often than not supervising production themselves, and sometimes embroidering on the craft tradition of furniture-makers, they are designing furniture that is breathing fresh life into British design. This category, which oscillates somewhere between art, craft, and industrial design, and is therefore difficult to pin down, is often designated by the names *artist-craftsmen* or *designer-makers*. Where does this wave come from, and what influence does it have? To what degree does it continue a British tradition of individualism and of loners operating beyond industrial reality?

Next on the agenda is the fashion revival. Not since the sixties have young radical fashion designers attracted so much international attention: London is back as a fashion centre. The graphic sector, by tradition a major field of British design, has made a name for itself too with countless new magazines and record sleeves. How close is the relationship of these innovations with the punk phenomenon – or with what in the United Kingdom is termed 'street style' or 'youth culture' – and what is its influence?

Together with the recent fields of television and pop music these developments give the impression that British design is at its strongest in the media-orientated areas where 'image' means everything. So by way of conclusion chapter ten takes a brief look at the pop video and advertising; on one hand because these fields are related to the more traditional design areas, on the other because Great Britain enjoys tremendous international prestige in both.

It is from these constants and variables in British design that this book has been written. It is an attempt to map out and explain them, aided by past developments and by the cultural values and traditions that have shaped British design. Just how new are these phenomena, and to what degree typically British? To put it another way: what constitutes the British identity in design?

On an island where they drive on the left instead of on the right, still refuse to measure distance in kilometres rather than miles, and find it difficult getting used to their EEC membership, you would expect products designed there to be quite out of the ordinary. What, then, gives British design its singularity? If German industrial design has a rational basis, Italian design is sensual, French inventive, and Scandinavian natural, then the words best applicable to industrial design in Britain are 'workmanlike' and 'solid'. If this is so, what are the reasons for it? This first chapter takes the form of a reconnaissance, a quest to explore in general terms the Britishness of British design, along with my first thoughts on the subject. In this chapter I shall be taking British product design as a vantage point from which to elicit what lies behind this solidity, and then to discover what other sides there may be to British design.

In her book *British Design since 1880, a visual history (1982)*, Fiona MacCarthy investigates the characteristics of British design. Words she uses to describe it are: sane and forthright, ordinary, solid, not extreme, honest, modest, homely, lacking sophistication, with very little feeling for the glamorous, reticent, and plain and simple. Frank Pick, who worked for the British Underground and in the thirties gave British design a tremendous boost, expressed it thus:

'Modest and not too grandiose in scale . . . not too logical in form . . . a reasonable compromise between beauty and utility, neither overstressing beauty till it degenerates into ornament, nor overstressing utility till it becomes bare and hard'.[1] Both emphasise its simplicity, lack of pretentiousness, and its reticence. So paradoxically enough, this unconventional island seems to spawn conventional product designs.

For the greater part of British design this to me seems indeed to be the case. Take the anything but revolutionary designs of Felix Summerly's Art Manufactures; the William Morris chairs steeped in the vernacular tradition; the sturdy-looking but fairly uninspired furniture of Heal's and Gordon Russell; the friendly, anecdotal – sometimes almost frumpish – tableware patterns of Eric Ravilious; the watered down modernism of the Habitat products; the undistinguished technical and electrical appliances of the sixties and seventies, now quite forgotten to us; the unoriginal chairs of Rodney Kinsman's OMK Design: and the innumerable middle-of-the-road, utterly acceptable designs by the big consultancies of the eighties.

CHAIR IN THE ADAM TRADITION, ABOUT 1775
carved and gilded wood, collection Norman Adam Ltd., London
Classical, elegant, and subtle

AC74 RADIO, 1933
Serge Chermayeff, E.K. Cole Ltd., phenolic resin

A22 RADIO, 1945
Wells Coates, E.K. Cole Ltd., phenolic resin

A culture without extremes

Why is it that so many British designs are moderate and so little extreme, never going too far, not very sophisticated, and, in general, not particularly subversive? Enquiry into this aspect of Britishness takes us for a large part to areas outside the limited one of design for an answer. Design is, after all, but a single component of a national culture that unavoidably shapes and influences it. We can better begin by looking at that aspect so cherished and loved by the British,

namely nature. The British landscape appears to have much in common with the products it spawns. In William Morris' marvellous description: 'Not much space for swelling into hugeness . . . no great wastes overwhelming in their dreariness, no great solitudes of forests, no terrible untrodden mountain walls; all is measured, mingled, varied, gliding easily one thing into another, little rivers, little plains . . . little hills, little mountains . . . neither prison, nor palace, but a decent home.'[2] Littleness and a decent home, and in a temperate climate too.

A second obvious direction in which to send out feelers is the British temperament. Although holding forth about a national disposition must be done with some caution, in general it can be said that extremes do not befit the British spirit. Properties like reticence and reservation are often attributed to the British. Then there is the language, which with its generous helping of monosyllables and its compact sentences gives evidence of an aversion to fuss and long-winded rhetoric. But then the British have no love of shooting straight from the hip – theirs is the language of the understatement.

In the history of the British visual arts, too, extremes are few and far between. There are portraits (Reynolds, Gainsborough), but no grand theatrical, mythological, or religious scenes. Nor does Britain offer fertile soil for the Baroque and the Rococo. There they prefer to stick to Classicism, or rather Palladianism. Nor is this just the result of the country's Protestantism, which, unlike Catholicism, has no love of outward display. Those in authority were just as averse to a surfeit of pomp and circumstance, and there was no urban elite to speak of. There are fine country houses in abundance, but no monumental town halls, *pallazi*, or *hôtels* as in other European seventeenth and eighteenth century cities; Arts and Crafts, but no Jugendstil and little Modern Movement; the Omega Group, but no bona fide Futurism, and no De Stijl. Currents that set art and design on the Continent on its head, caused nary a ripple in insular Britain.

Exceptional geniuses comparable to a Giotto, Michelangelo, or a Rembrandt are a rarity in British fine art: Turner is perhaps the only one. Nikolaus Pevsner, whose keen observation produced a clear and stimulating book entitled *The Englishness of English Art* (still relevant thirty-two years later), relates this to the amateur and to conservatism.[3] According to him traditions are never violated, let alone ditched entirely. Moderation and evolution are in general much more at home in British art than is extremism.

Nor does British history testify either to bloody revolutions that shook the country to its foundations. The Glorious Revolution of 1688 was neither a revolution nor glorious. It gave England a Protestant monarchy and confirmed the sovereignty of Parliament, but it was no sudden, violent seizure of power, no social upheaval.[4]

Nor did the turbulent sixties of our own century in Britain have anything like the far-reaching social consequences that they had in, say, France or West Germany. The power structure remained essentially unaffected, and with it the authority of the establishment. The rather inflexible British class system was never really breached, and so here, too, continuity and tradition prevail.

The term 'moderation' also contains something of compromise, of not daring to adopt an extreme standpoint. Professor Bernard

RADIO, 1934
Misha Black, E.K. Cole Ltd., phenolic resin

TOKYO, 1988
Nigel Coates NATO (Narrative Architecture Today)

Crick traces this British characteristic back to English history when toleration and compromise were political tactics. By permitting the cultural plurism of Wales, Scotland, and Ireland the central power remained safe from threat.[5] The British Empire too was kept under control more by diplomacy than by violence. Also, the British two-party political system strengthened the inclination towards tolerance and compromise. In a multitude of respects the moderation of British product design, I feel, has its roots firmly entrenched in British culture.

A rational approach to design

Besides factors from outside, those inside the profession offer their own explanation for the middle-of-the-road quality of designing. The British design approach in particular says much about the products which stem from it. Pragmatics is a constantly recurring theme here. As the *Art Journal* observed more than a century ago: 'Give an Englishman a definite purpose to accomplish, and do not fetter him with rules of art wholly inapplicable to the case, and he will imagine something as new as the exigency; rendered beautiful by that exact coincidence between the end and the means which affects the senses with the same sort of satisfaction the solution of a problem gives to the mind.'[6] It concluded that building for utility was closer to an Englishman's heart than building for decoration. This is evidenced not only by Paxton's Crystal Palace, but by untold other engineer's architecture of that century. The pragmatics of technology were better suited to the British than was taste.[7] In British architecture the useful and factual tie in with a rationality inherited from the Classicist, Palladian tradition. Geometry and pragmatics were to return in the Brutalist architecture of the fifties, and High-Tech too is characterised by an interest in construction.

In 1847 Felix Summerly's Art Manufactures, the group of designers and artists around Henry Cole, proclaimed its intention 'to revive the good old practice of connecting the best art with familiar objects in daily use. In doing this Art Manufactures will aim to

SPITTING IMAGE

produce in each article superior utility, which is not to be sacrificed to ornament.'[8] Here the emphasis is very much on usefulness and an everyday quality. The DIA (Design and Industries Association, founded in 1915) proclaimed 'fitness for purpose' as its ideal. The postwar Design Council also considered good, solid, and useable design to be of paramount importance. 'We should approach each new problem from the base of practicality', urged the designer and professor Misha Black as late as 1975.[9]

The British approach to design is one of common sense, rooted

JAGUAR
collection The British Motor Industry Heritage Trust
Well groomed, tame and well mannered

in the actual making (the craft tradition). It is intuitive, or 'doing-as-designing'. 'Here designing is based on practice, not on philosophy', says Floris van den Broecke, designer and professor at the Royal College of Art.[10] And so in Britain there is no articulation of a theoretical design ideology. Coherent theories with a socio-political undercurrent comparable to Futurism, De Stijl, Constructivism, and the Bauhaus are to all intents and purpose nonexistent.
Designers rarely express themselves through design movements or streams. Their ideology is more implicit. Individualism, handed down by the traditional, craft-based foundations of British design, is all-dominating. What is more, thinking about the future, anticipating it, and experimenting with it as happens in Italy and Japan is – unlike in British architecture – seldom come across amongst Britain's designers.

The graphic tradition

Another explanation of the moderation in British design may be the strong graphic tradition permeating it in a multitude of ways, beginning with William Morris' interest in lettering and the book. His Kelmscott Press breathed fresh life into book design, and this influence spread by way of designers like Edward Johnston and Eric Gill. The linear and two-dimensional can be discovered elsewhere in British culture, such as in medieval church construction, which has little of the spatial and sculptural. The nineteenth century engineers' architecture and High-Tech buildings of our own day are also characterised by a certain linearity. Alan Fletcher of Pentagram design consultancy argues that British graphic design is in addition influenced by calligraphy, heraldry, and folk art.[11]

The decorative, folklore-based element is clearly present in products of the Art and Crafts movement too. British Art and Crafts practitioners excelled in textiles and wallpaper, where they give evidence of their capabilities on a flat surface. Britain is also very strong in fields like illustration. The second dimension, with its literary, narrative quality, seems much more suited to British designers than the third. So the supposition that British design is

RADIO, 1948
R.D. Russell, Murphy Radio Ltd., walnut

average, sound, and nonextreme might then have something to do with a lack of feeling for the three-dimensional.

Devoid of expression?

Commonsense and rationality are very much at odds with imagination and the emotions. Have the British learnt to suppress their personal identity at public schools and in clubs, as the designer

Wally Olins claims?[12] Anthony Sampson contends that such institutions turn out individuals who are intellectually overdeveloped and emotionally underdeveloped.[13] 'The strongly puritanical streak in British society', says design critic John Thackara, 'distrusts sensuality, individualism and artistic expression.'[14] The designer as genius or star is unheard of in Britain, as against postwar Finland or Italy. Nor is art anywhere near the centre of attention: talents in this field are not encouraged. As the fashion designer John Galliano complains: 'Designers are pretty well treated like children in England . . . We're not treated with the respect we should be.'[15] Should we then fear the worst for British design?

That remains to be seen, as simplicity and modesty have led to

CORONATION MUG, 1937
Eric Ravilious, Wedgwood
This mug, designed for the coronation of Edward VIII and adapted for that of George VI and, in 1953, that of Queen Elizabeth II, reveals Ravilious' background as a book illustrator

VASE, 18TH CENTURY
Wedgwood, black basalt, collection Boymans-van Beuningen Museum, Rotterdam
Black basalt is a dense black stoneware of extreme hardness that shows no trace of the maker's touch

extremely powerful British designs with a poise that commands respect. Examples include Wedgwood pottery; Chippendale and Queen Anne furniture; metalwork by Christopher Dresser; textiles and wallpaper by William Morris; glass by Philip Webb for Powell; pottery by Keith Murray; the graphic design for the London Undergound; the Jaguar; David Mellor's cutlery; The *Lloyd* chair of Jane Dillon, Floris van den Broecke, and Peter Wheeler.
Their strength often lies in a powerful, almost obvious design of an associative and subtle nature. In it the linear and the plastic are in perfect equilibrium. The words which express this British quality best are elegant and subtle. Here, British individuality, intimate but not obtrusive, is, I feel, at its most pervasive. The Boilerhouse catalogue *National Characteristics in Design* compares British design – and how much more British can a comparison get? – with a racehorse: 'Well groomed . . . tame and well mannered.'[16] Here pragmatics, tolerance, and compromise are welded into a potent synthesis.

Graphic design is an exception in another way to the characteristics outlined above. In fact it attests to an amazing capacity for digesting foreign influences. Swiss and Dutch typography were important new stimuli on prewar British graphics, and foreign designers settling in Britain enriched further the British graphic tradition. The result is a tremendous diversity. Here the pragmatic side of British culture is a great advantage.

Pragmatic, in the final analysis, does not mean dogmatic, but 'every case on its own merit'. In general the British designer avoids being cramped by rules and principles and in his stand-offishness is less inclined to prejudice. The landscape gardens of the eighteenth century – informal, varied, and not laid out according to inflexible rules – are a good example of this. Compulsory mechanised production and Functionalism are largely misunderstood in the United Kingdom. 'Consistency as a good idea scarcely exists here', according to Floris van den Broecke.[17] The lack of dogmatism renders British culture more pluralistic and allows for a greater variety of ideas. There is also a tendency towards irony to be found in graphics and advertising. We could say, then, that the supposition that British design is average, respectable, and nonextreme is only true in part.

ANTELOPE CHAIR, 1951
Ernest Race, Race Furniture Ltd., steel rod, moulded plywood seat
This chair was made for the Festival of Britain of 1951
and reflects the postwar optimism

Extremes

The unavoidable conclusion we can draw from this initial reconnaissance of the Britishness of British design is that it – and

PRIDE CUTLERY, 1954
designed and produced by David Mellor, silverplated, xylonite
collection Boymans-van Beuningen Museum, Rotterdam, gift from the designer
A classic design still in production

British culture in general – is not without its paradoxes. On one hand there is the insularity of a Britain repelling foreign influences; on the other, the presence of a remarkable number of foreign designers who have made a considerable impression on British design, like Misha Black, Edward McKnight Kauffer, Serge Chermayeff, and F.H.K. Henrion. British design is useful and factual, but romantic (the craft tradition) and decorative too; there is personal expression and pragmatic compromise; individualism and conformism; but it is also nonextreme and at the same time very much extreme.

The last-named contradiction has been at its most prominent during the last twenty-five years. Tradition is constantly being challenged by eccentric, largely individualist counteractions. Besides professional documentaries by the BBC there are satirical programmes on television like *That Was The Week That Was*, *Monty Python's Flying Circus*, and *Spitting Image*. Along with Georgian architecture we find the *Instant City* of Archigram, not to mention the chaos of NATO; *House & Garden* and *Private Eye, The Independent* and the tabloids. The United Kingdom is not only the land of hand-made Saville Row suits, but that of Pop, Punk, and Vivienne Westwood; from Shetland woollies to what author Peter York describes as the 'Oh-my-God-I'd-never-wear-it' future. In the field of furniture innovatory designer-makers, unarguably a fringe phenomenon, are promoting a sort of punk aesthetics by working with unwrought metal, jagged glass, and rough concrete. In doing so, designers like Ron Arad, Danny Lane, and Nigel Coates are challenging the established furniture industry, which has produced nothing of note for decades on end. In fields like advertising, graphics, and video, which surveys of British design tend to ignore, we can see similar extremes. The eccentricity seems to me at all events something typically British, because of the very ubiquity of tradition there. Pevsner observes that the British have a long tradition as cartoonists.[18] He links this to the tendency to moralise which is very much present in British art. I wonder whether these often humorous counteractions have something to do with a high degree of tolerance, a British respect for the individual, and a tradition of dissent. Individualism is in itself a trait deeply entrenched in Britain.

CROWS FOOT DECANTER, 1879
Christopher Dresser, Hukin & Heath, silverplated, glass, collection Boymans-van Beuningen Museum, Rotterdam

The historian Alan Macfarlane asserts that the notion of private, individually owned property has, unlike in other countries, existed in England at least since the thirteenth century.[19] David Marquand calls the Glorious Revolution in a politico-administrative sense a victory of squires over royalty, and from this concludes that in Britain it was not the State, but individuals and institutes who led the process of

PADDED GARMENT, 1988
Georgina Godley

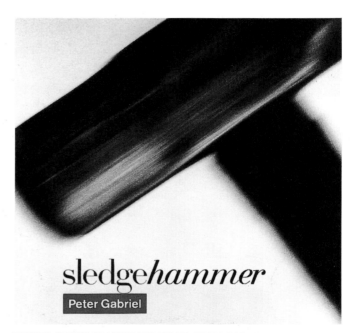

RECORD SLEEVE FOR SLEDGEHAMMER, PETER GABRIEL, 1986
Peter Saville Associates/Trevor Key

modernisation.[20] There is also the tradition of the amateur to consider.

British eccentricity, on the other hand, seems to me to possess distinct, though admittedly undefined, rules. Criticism wrapped in humour, harmless enough in itself, is tolerated; not so protest of a more threatening nature, which is 'not cricket'. The nineteenth century middle classes who at first snapped up all William Morris' creations with glee soon turned against him when he emerged as a revolutionary activist. Morris was upbraided for being a 'misguided idealist' and a 'poet-upholsterer'.[21] The fate of the writer and dandy Oscar Wilde is another example of British hypocrisy in this respect. And recently a batch of new British films, praised outside the British Isles for the harrowing picture they present of Thatcher's England, were given a mauling by the British press. *Sammie and Rosie Get Laid, The Last of England, Eat the Rich, Empire State, Business as Usual* – these were seized on by the British press and ruthlessly dragged through the mud. 'At last an original', exclaimed Mrs. Thatcher at a cocktail

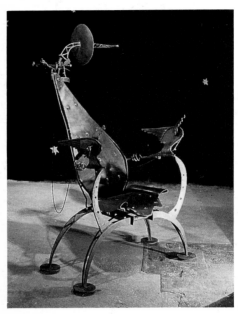

DAN DARE CHAIR, 1987
Jon Mills, metal
challenging the established furniture industry
with a sort of punk aesthetics

party to the woman entering wearing a t-shirt bearing the legend '58% don't want Pershing'. The woman was the fashion designer Katharine Hamnett, the cocktail party was at No. 10 Downing Street in honour of British fashion, and at it Hamnett tackled the Prime Minister on the problems of acid rain (not cricket at all!). Eccentrics are popular, and intriguing – could this be snobbery? – but should behave like the amateurs they are, and above all keep their distance!

Tradition, as I see is, is the pivot around which British culture revolves, including the reactions against it in the form of shocking or

humorous eccentricity. These reactions are as sharp as the tradition they challenge is strong. British design oscillates between these two poles of tradition and eccentricity. According to Peter York Britain's two prime specialities are punk and pageantry. The British pop video is for him the ultimate example of what present-day British design is about. 'They're all about dressing up and making up and playing around. They call on the past and the future in a fantastical, ironic way. They're about dreams, they're like dreams, full of ambiguities and gender-confusion – another British triumph – and of course jokes.'[22] This aspect of Britishness, once again, will also be discussed at greater length in the chapters to follow.

ARMCHAIR, 1985
Mary Little, batch produced by Mary Little, wood on a steel tube frame
This much-pulicised chair was Mary Little's student project
in her final year at the RCA

chapter two   **ENGLAND AS THE GARDEN**

Nowhere were the principles of mechanical production applied so early and so systematically as in Britain, who with her Industrial Revolution led the rest of the world. New materials and sources of energy were tapped; the steam engine and new manufacturing processes made possible the mass production of iron and textiles. The enterprising Josiah Wedgwood was one of the first manufacturers to use to the full both the division of labour and standardisation, and to recognise the importance of the designer, who provided him with new models and decorations. The legendary Crystal Palace with its standardised elements prefabricated in industrial materials with the aid of an abundance of new, ingenious, and time-saving machinery represented the crowning glory of capitalist attainment. The Britain of the centuries preceding our own seems to have been bristling with brilliant minds whose inventions and innovations astonished the world and looked to the future.

But, beside the image of Great Britain as the Workshop of the World, there exists an equally persistent picture handed down through the ages of England as the Garden. It is inhabited not by industrialists and inventors, but by gentlemen and poets. Here there is no machinery humming, nor astounding feats of technology, but country houses, gardens, and craftsmen. These two worlds, which I will be discussing in the following two chapters, were not infrequently at loggerheads with one another. Why was this, and what effect did it have on the British design climate which was influenced by the Industrial Revolution on one hand, and rooted in crafts ideals on the other? So let us take a look at the rural tradition of Great Britain and its influence.

Gentlemen and social climbers

The rural tradition, most clearly symbolised by the gentleman in his country house, is bound up with a mentality that evolved through the ages and influenced all branches of British society until well into this century. Although the rustic idyllic image of England as 'the garden' has helped sell many British products abroad, others see it more in terms of anti-industrial values. Particularly in the last few years historians have been focusing attention on these cultural values which, in a country where continuity and tradition are held in high esteem, help to explain the specific attitude of the British to their industrial culture. The tremendous charm that glorious England exerts particularly on foreigners is seen by the British as a stumbling-block to a modern economy. From this recent literature the most important sustainer of the anti-industrial culture seems to have been the upper classes. These remained extremely influential in many areas, permeating British society with their values until well into this century.

For centuries the political power of this homogeneous and stable elite was rooted in landed property. But, while displaying verve and a spirit of innovative enterprise in improving agricultural methods and transport routes, it had no intention at all of involving itself with the nouveau riche of the business world. The hitherto prevailing assumption that this elite merged effortlessly and without a struggle with the nouveau riche, through which Britain led the field in the Industrial Revolution, is a myth. This is evidenced by recent research by, amongst others, Stone and Fawtier-Stone.[1] They conclude that '. . . the contemporary perceptions and conventional historical wisdom about the exceptional freedom of interchange between land and money amongst the English elite are not borne out by the statistical facts, either about land and seats purchased by the urban patriciate, or about personal, marital, or family ties back one generation among owners of landed estates and seats, or even – . . .–about the entry of younger sons into business.'[2] They are of the opinion that 'the unity of English elite society was a unity of the land and the professions, only marginally of the land and business, and not at all of land and industry.'[3] Although the historian Tom Nairn equates the powerful position of the gentry with their liaison with City capital, what Stone and Fawtier-Stone mean here is a social integration, or rather non-integration.[4]

The distinction between land and industry was in previous ages embodied in the concept of the gentleman, who was more interested in prestige than in profit. His was a life of leisure, in which work was a pleasant pastime.[5] This ties in once again with the British predilection for the amateur. Cited by Stone and Fawtier-Stone as the most important characteristics of the country squire are an '. . . education in the classics, and the pursuit of a life of elegant ease and leisure based primarily in the countryside. But there was more to him than that. He was also a virtuoso, an admirer of aesthetic beauty

WILLIAM MORRIS AND THE SOCIALIST LEAGUE

in art, architecture and gardens, a defender of traditions and the rights of birth, and (in theory) a conscientious paternalist ruler of the countryside.'[6]

In Britain this contradiction seems to have been effortlessly assimilated because the urban businessmen, the middling sort, and the industrialists all aspired to the gentleman's status and adopted his lifestyle and values. Nineteenth century Britain apparently had an aristocratic bourgeoisie rather than a bourgeois aristocracy. Moreover, a powerful middle class was always lacking, and the country elite had no urban counterbalance. The gentry's antipathy towards industry and industrial values infiltrated the most important social institutions. From the nineteenth century onwards, members of the rural upper classes predominated in such bastions as banks and offices, the Church, the universities, the army, the Colonies, and the government. Around 1900, for example, G.B. Dibbee wrote that the '. . . best brains of our upper classes will go anywhere but into industry – into a bank or a merchants office perhaps, but not into horny-handed manufacture.'[7]

The conservative elite looked down on industry, creating a divided nation which has been described by a pair of contrasting metaphors. 'In the Northern Metaphor Britain is pragmatic, empirical, calculating, Puritan, bourgeois, enterprising, adventurous, scientific, serious, and believes in struggle. Its sinful excess is a ruthless avarice, rationalised in the belief that the prime impulse in all human beings is a rational, calculating economic self-interest. In the Southern Methapor, Britain is romantic, illogical, muddled, divinely lucky, Anglican, aristocratic, frivolous, and believes in order and tradition. Its sinful excess is a ruthless pride, rationalised in the belief that men are born to serve.'[8]

According to Martin Wiener, author of a book on British anti-industrial culture, the Southern Metaphor triumphed at the beginning of the twentieth century over the Northern, giving rise to the notion that British success was due not to effort, but to its unique cultural

ASHBEE AT CHIPPING CAMPDEN
Away from the complex, artificial and often destructive influences of machinery and the great town

heritage. 'Just when, after World War I, the role of government was gaining major importance for the national economy, government and politics had become permeated by a mentality that regarded industry as a necessary evil and innovation and competition as risky and not quite reputable,' says Wiener, who also speaks of 'a nation, and an elite, at war with itself.'[9] The historian and politician David P. Marquand claims that the British were unable to shake off their nineteenth century values because these had made their country what it was.[10]

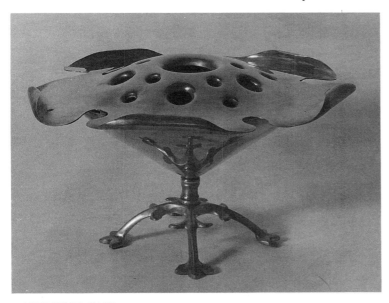

FLOWER STAND, C 1890
W.A.S. Benson, metal

The problem still existed in 1986 when those organising the British Industry Year said that Britain was suffering from 'self-inflicted wounds' caused by 'a set of attitudes, culture and education which lead society to put industry at the bottom of our social pecking order.'[11] A recent investigation by *The Economist* confirmed that 32% of Oxbridge students 'were put off jobs in industry because they thought they were low-status or dirty.'[12]

RUSH-SEATED CHAIR, 1865
William Morris, Morris, Marshall, Faulkner & Co., ebonised beech
collection Victoria and Albert Museum, London
Its design is based on that of the vernacular Sussex chair

DINNER PLATE, 1913
hand-painted by Roger Fry of Omega

A Trojan horse?

While the clash of country and industry was manifested in a comparatively indirect way amongst the ranks of the gentlemen, the

¼ size

INTERIOR, KELMSCOTT MANOR
William Morris

HOVIS COMMERCIAL
Collett, Dickenson, Pearce and Partners Ltd.

opposition amongst artists was far more pronounced. Writers, poets, painters, architects, and designers found it difficult to come to terms with modern industrial society. This was at its most apparent at the time of the Great Exhibition of 1851, which brought these differences of opinion into the open.

'In the temple raised to the Industry of all Nations by our Queen and her illustrious Consort, we see the unquestioned evidence of the march of intellect, and of its incalculable advantages over the tramp of war; we see how times and feelings change; we learn to estimate the 'peaceful arts' and the numerous blessings they engender; we see how perfect and how beautiful is the chain of civilisation . . .'[13] 'The productions of every land are there; every thing, whether mineral, vegetable, or animal, which man has applied either to useful ends or ornamental purposes, is gathered together to tell its own tale of the luxuriant wealth of Nature and of the powers of the human mind.'[14] In its day, the overwhelming Great Exhibition

embodied the triumph of mind over matter, the all-conquering industrialisation process. Humanistic optimism had reached a peak. Prince Albert, 'the industrious boy', and driving force behind this ambitious operation, praised in his inaugural speech the attainments of the New Age. He represented the feelings of euphoria prevalent in the Western world regarding modern life. '. . . the great principle of division of labour, which may be called the moving power of civilisation, is being extended to all branches of science, industry and art . . . the products of all quarters of the globe, are placed at our disposal, and we have only to choose which is the best and cheapest for our purpose, and the powers of production are entrusted to the stimulus of competition and capital. So man is approaching a more complete fulfilment of that great and sacred mission which he has to perform in the world.'[15] Entirely in the spirit of the theory of evolution Albert saw the division of labour as a vehicle for still greater achievements. In this optimistic vision, competition and capital, in other words the entrepreneurs, functioned as stimulants to industry which in turn stood for the universal, for civilisation, and for progress. It represented a world without borders, the free exchange of ideas, and the conquest of new markets. To the urban middle class of that time the principles of supply and demand were seen as God-given. Prince Albert: 'His [man's] reason being created after the image of God, he has to use it to discover the laws by which the Almighty governs his creation, and by making his laws his standard of action to conquer nature to his use, – himself a divine instrument.'[16]

Yet in spite of all the optimism, it transpired that Britain had taken in a Trojan horse, for in the very year of Albert's jubilant opening address, the seeds of opposition were already seen to be germinating. Thus John Ruskin criticised the division of labour in his book *The Stones of Venice (1851)*: 'We have much studied, and much perfected, of late, the great civilized invention of the division of labour; only we gave it a false name. It is not, truly speaking, the labour that is divided; but the men: – divided into mere segments of men – broken into small fragments and crumbs of life; so that all the piece of intelligence that is left in a man is not enough to make a pin,

40

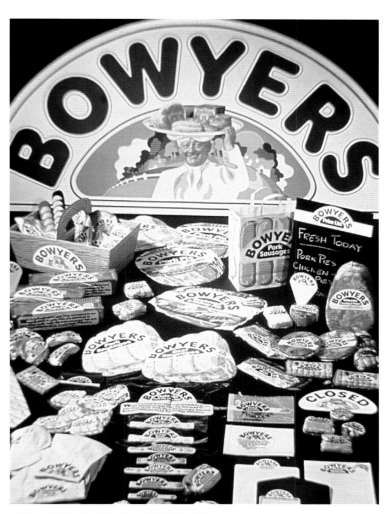

CORPORATE IDENTITY FOR BOWYER'S, 1970
Wolff Olins
An early example of the use of rural imagery to sell foodstuffs

or a nail, but exhausts itself in making the point or the head of a nail.'[17]

His was not the only criticism. Other intellectuals too greeted progress and the industrialisation of Victorian Britain with feelings that were not entirely positive. Although not constituting a powerful counterforce – until about 1870 the word 'intellectual' did not refer to a member of a social group – they were quite unanimous in their rejection of industrial culture. Writers, artists, architects, and designers reacted violently to the domination of utilitarian and commercial values which came with capitalism and the march of science. Art, imagination, and emotion were under siege, as they saw it.

Romantic revolt

The Romantic poets (Keats, Shelley, Wordsworth, Blake) felt seriously threatened. Fired by nostalgia for the values capitalism had destroyed, Keats intensified his predilection for the Middle Ages. For him poetry was a flight from harsh reality, from which he withdrew to devote himself to art alone. Writers like John Stuart Mill, Matthew Arnold, Anthony Trollope, Charles Dickens, and Thomas Carlyle expressed in their books a growing repugnance for the social system. Dickens, in *Hard Times*, wrote: 'The school was all fact, and the school of design was all fact, and the relations between master and man were all fact, and everything was fact between the lying-in hospital and the cemetery, and what you couldn't state in figures, or show to be purchasable in the cheapest market and salable in the dearest, was not, and never should be, world without end, amen.'[18] 'A society based upon cash and self-interest is not a society at all, but a state of war', to cite Carlyle who was attacking the individualist character of liberalism.[19] He offered life in a monastery as an example of the right approach.

The unfurled standard of the Romantic Revolt was passed on by literature into the hands of artists and architects. The Pre-Raphaelites revolted against the prevalent artistic climate and academic art. Instead of mannered, formal landscapes, portraits, and

genre paintings they advocated the honesty of painting directly from nature and the autonomy of art (l'art pour l'art). Their argument was for personal, individual (emotional) expression; their dream was the creation of Great Art as compensation for harsh reality.
Their reaction, one of retreat and rejection, was a defensive one.

The young William Morris joined this Pre-Raphaelite Brotherhood opting, however, for a more direct confrontation not only by taking over the production of objects for use himself, but also as a militant socialist. 'Apart from the desire to produce beautiful things, the leading passion of my life has been and is hatred of modern civilisation.'[20]

Arts and Crafts

And yet the association Morris evokes of a 'daydreaming hater of machinery' has persisted. Even in 1979 the director of the Design Museum in London speaking of Morris and his circle evoked a stereotyped image in 'the promise of a pseudo-medieval fantasy world, populated by bearded epic poets sitting on expensive reproduction furniture.'[21] But William Morris' protest was in no way directed at the machine. On the contrary, he saw it as an instrument and as a liberating force. 'It is the allowing of machines to be our masters, and not our servants, that so injures the beauty of life nowadays.'[22] And the same goes for the fantasy world accusation: 'We cannot turn our image of a people back into catholic English peasants and guild craftsmen or into heathen Norse bonders, much as can be said for such conditions of life.'[23] The picture of a daydreaming hater of machinery is, as the historian E.P. Thompson convincingly shows, an unjustifiable one.[24] But because Morris is chiefly known through his book *News from Nowhere*, where he is less explicit than in his lectures, this remains the overriding opinion.

He opposed the division of labour through mechanisation which from the end of the sixteenth century onwards had produced a division into 'fine' and 'applied' art (mental creations versus wage labour), and had given the world autonomous art. It seems, therefore,

GARDEN CITY, 1882

that intellectual reactions in the century preceding our own should be seen not so much as anti-industrial, but far more as anti-capitalist.[25] Martin Wiener suggests that with the mid-nineteenth century there came a counter-revolution in values which he considers the principal cause of the economic recession that in Britain lived on into the twentieth century.[26] He points to, amongst other things, the British predilection for the past and idealisation of things rural, and cites cases reaching far into the second half of this century. In his view the British themselves saw Britain less as 'the workshop of the world' than as 'the garden'.

That also held true for the Arts and Crafts designers themselves. Not so much because they were nostalgic, excessively concerned with the past, unworldy, and inclined to romanticise – the time-honoured cliché applied to Morris crops up in Wiener's case too – but above all because, united in guilds and following Morris' example, they made their home in the country. Ruskin and the members of the Arts and Crafts movement saw nature as the diametrical opposite of industry: ' . . . the proper place for the Arts and Crafts is in the country . . . away from the complex, artificial and often destructive influences of machinery and the great town.'[27] C.R. Ashbee, whose statement this is, believed in the machine, while hoping nevertheless that the revival of craftmanship would influence manufacturers and public taste.[28] Macfarlane explains the British love of nature as a reaction to utilitarian capitalism and links this to anti-urban values and to the elite who sought not the town but the country.[29] The garden city was to become Britain's most prominent contribution to architecture and town planning. The work of Norman

VASE, WILLIAM DE MORGAN

Shaw and Ebenezer Howard laid the foundations for the garden city movement which at the beginning of this century was given shape in Letchworth (1903) and Welwyn (1919). Architects like Philip Webb and Charles Voysey built in a sort of local cottage style. Even now the majority of British craftsmen, and a few designers like John Makepeace, David Mellor and Robert Welch, work and live in the country.

Arts and Crafts traditions left their mark for a long time on British design. Not just because of British conservatism and the predilection for upholding tradition, but chiefly because its practitioners in their artists' colonies were completely detached from industry. These two worlds were light years apart, not least because the Arts and Crafts designers themselves came from elite circles where industrialists were treated with disdain. Most industrialists, on the other hand, were rooted in rural workmanship.

Thus the Design and Industries Association or DIA, set up in 1915, while based on the German Werkbund with its vigorous promotion of industrial design, showed little of this in practice. Here too it seems that conservatism and defensive behaviour prevailed at the cost of enterprise and initiative; any confrontation with a problem is neatly sidestepped. Standardisation and mass production in the hands of British designers did not, as it did with their foreign colleagues, lead to heated discussions. The Modern Movement, which reached its zenith on the Continent, made little headway in Britain. 'It must be remembered', confirms Gordon Russell, designer and later director of the CoID, in his autobiography *Designer's Trade,* 'that in the 1920's no school of art, as far as I am aware, had accepted the principle that designing for the machine needed a very different training from designing for hand production. Most of the schools were in charge of painters, who cradled in Arts and Crafts Society theories, were antagonistic to industry and did not hesitate to say so. Industry naturally reacted by ignoring their existence.'[30] Consequently there was, prior to the Second World War, no integration of industrialists and designers of any consequence. It was more a case of isolated incidents and exceptions than that of a solid basis laid to sustain development of the profession.

BIRD TEXTILE, 1878
William Morris, woven wool
collection Boymans-van Beuningen Museum, Rotterdam

Schools and scientists

Education and science together formed a third bearer of anti-industrial values. From early on, Britain's public schools and universities were geared to the upper classes. They doggedly maintained the values of the gentleman despite several brave attempts to introduce reform. While the world around them was rapidly and drastically changing, they clung to an educational programme based on the classics and mathematics. Oxford, Cambridge, and all other such institutes of higher learning in their romantically rural settings, continued to embrace such values as the team spirit as opposed to individual action, clinging to tradition rather than a utilitarian rationalism, and hierarchy instead of social equality. 'They were

friendly neither to creative imagination nor to innovation generally. They looked upon business as a fundamentally crass and ungentlemanly occupation.'[31] 'England remained remarkably committed to values and attitudes discouraging to science, even while science advanced in knowledge, organisation and professional status,' according to the historian Heyck.[32]

In the days when Britain led the world with countless scientific discoveries, the application of these, paradoxically enough, failed to realise their full potential. The scientists themselves were well aware of the inadequately low level of education in their field, and complained that science was not an organised profession. But, generally of middle-class background, they too became bitten by the status bug and aspired to the position of gentleman. Universities that were less central, and more directly linked with the industries, also modelled themselves more and more on the Oxbridge example. The government, used to a Liberal, individualist laissez-faire ideology, saw no reason to encourage science or give it some sort of structure. The Royal Society, for instance, was until 1847 not led by scientists actively engaged, and seemed more a grand gentlemen's club than an enterprising, active, and stimulating institute.

The status of the British scientist remained low. 'A man of science', complained the biologist T.H. Huxley in 1901, 'may earn great distinction, but not bread.'[33] His French and German colleagues, on the other hand, were held in high system. In these countries knowledge and titles mean status. There, talent and competition were the cornerstones of an intellectual culture, and making science a useful commodity had a higher priority. French intellectuals also involve themselves more with the social and political system. Even today scientists feel isolated, outsiders cut off from the rest of the British echelons of power, divided among themselves into rival institutes and organisations, and operating in the no-man's-land between conservatives and those with an eye to the future. This is further evident from recent complaints by engineers like Peter Rice and Tony Hunt, who gained distinction with their work on impressive High-Tech buildings. ' . . . it *is* important that the public perception of engineers should be improved,' says Peter Rice

WINE LABEL FOR ASDA WINES & SPIRITS, 1987-88
art director, Mary Lewis, designer, Lucy Drew
Lewis Moberly Design Consultants

HIGHLAND MALT WHISKY LABEL FOR ASDA WINES & SPIRITS, 1987-88
Mary Lewis of Lewis Moberly Design Consultants

of the Ove Arup Partnership. 'In France and Germany, engineering has a very hig status, the best schools are the engineering schools, and the best people go into engineering. Here they don't.'[34] 'After all, look at the engineering profession itself – some 40 different institutions cater for and dispute its needs, and if we can't get together with ourselves, I don't know who we can get together with,' adds Tony Hunt.[35]

The postwar research institutes set up by Harold Wilson seemed too official, too slow-moving, and too unwilling to take risks. The vast amount of money used for research into defence and aeronautics failed to result in the commercial exploitation of knowledge. The *Comet Aircraft* (1954), the *Blue Streak* missile system (1961), and the supersonic *Concorde* (1976) all came to grief, and at that time contributed nothing towards strengthening the country's

**COUNTRY MEETING OF THE ROYAL
AGRICULTURAL SOCIETY OF ENGLAND AT BRISTOL, 1842**
painted by Richard Ansdell, collection City Gallery Salford

competitive position economically. Pioneers of the first generation of computers, the British lost this prominent role in the fifties and sixties.

Another substantial problem was the fluctuations in British politics resulting from a system in which each new government can easily reverse decisions taken by its predecessor. Thus Edward Heath could abolish the Industrial Reorganisation Corporation set up in 1966 by Wilson. During the Thatcher administration the National Enterprise Board (NEB) has had to put up with cuts. She, too, in turn created from existing institutes the British Technology Group (BTG) established to link research done at universities to industry. 'Present policies do not favour a change of heart in society's attitudes to engineering and to its practitioners. Educational cuts, recessional policies of short-term value but long-term danger, and the aggressive industrial trading of competitive countries do not encourage the talents of our engineering cadre' was the conclusion of an investigation among engineers in 1983.[36] Again, the Colleges of Advanced Technology, promoted in the sixties to universities, and the Polytechnics created by the Labour

government would undergo drastic cuts two decades later.

In companies the selfsame reticence prevails as regards investment in new technologies, given exceptions. The problem is 'one of fear of failure in the use of technology, more than fear that the finance is not available.'[37] The budget for Research and Development in private companies increased in Britain by just 6% in 1986, against an average of 32% in other countries.[38] In this respect it should be remembered that in the period when the government was pumping capital into fundamental research, which has no direct application in industry, complaints about the lack of applied research were flying thick and fast, whereas now with Mrs. Thatcher at the helm advocating this very research it is the state of fundamental research which elicits noises of discontent.[39]

It does seem as if anything new in science and technology is generally greeted in Britain with adverse criticism, and regarded as a threat. Reactions to, say, the rise of Japan are sooner defensive than enterprising. Thus *Design* could state quite recently that 'British manufacturers missed the microwave oven bandwagon and *allowed* the Japanese *to come in and steal* their home market.' (my italics)[40] The designer Kenneth Grange talks about 'a Japanese plot going on, to take over by the year 2000.'[41] Although this particularly unenterprising stance has undoubtedly done much to strengthen the anti-industrial culture, Britain has, on the other hand, a respectable tradition of inventions and entrepreneurial activity. How can this paradox be explained?

chapter three   **THE WORKSHOP OF THE WORLD**

Despite the prevailing image of England as the Garden, Great Britain nevertheless has an impressive tradition as regards entrepreneurs and inventions. In 1709 Abraham Darby used coke for smelting iron instead of the increasingly scarce coal. In doing so he laid the basis for the production of wrought iron on a large scale. The steam engine, invented by Thomas Newcomen and perfected by James Watt, helped to bring about the factory. People who had formerly worked at home became factory employers, and industrial centres sprang up. Textile manufacture in particular became mechanised at a rapid pace as the inventions came thick and fast: John Kay's flying shuttle of 1733, James Hargreaves' spinning Jenny of 1767, and Richard Arkwright's water frame of 1775.[1] Machine production made possible the quarrying and processing of raw materials on a large scale, and, in turn, encouraged industrial activity amongst suppliers and manufacturers of components.

Between 1830 and 1848 British iron production rose by no less than 300%, as against an increase of 65% in France between 1830 and 1845; in that last year the German states did not even manage a tenth of the British production.[2] In 1848 Britain's coal production made up two-thirds, and that of cotton more than half, of the world total.[3] This was enough to earn Britain the nickname 'the workshop of the world'. What formed the basis of this glorious industrial past, and in what form has it continued into our own century? To answer this question, this chapter takes a look at Britain's entrepreneurs, its industrial and economic history, and today's enterprise culture of Margaret Thatcher.

The industrial culture of the entrepreneurs

From 1750 onwards, Great Britain took up its position as a world leader. This was due in part to its wealth of raw materials, a comparative stability with little social unrest and virtually no wars, a Liberal government, and few powerful guilds. Over and above that, the country emerged as an enormous free trade area with a highly-developed banking system in which capital needed to be invested. As opposed to a country like France, where since the eighteenth century economic activity was stimulated by an absolutist, centralised monarchy whose enlightened kings proudly proclaimed themselves servers of the state, the British royal house, or State, here played only a secondary role. After the country-based elite had defeated the Stuarts it was individuals and institutions who were the bearers of all

CALICO PRINTING
mechanisation arouna 1835

things modern. A tough line on the economy coming from the state itself was entirly lacking.[4] In this respect the historian Klemm cites as example the Puritans and Quakers, who with their ethics of hard work and practical disposition did much to promote technological progress and free enterprise.[5] Thus as early as 1754 the Society for the Encouragement of Arts, Manufactures, and Commerce was founded by private individuals. The liberalist laissez-faire policy only served to strengthen private enterprise.

Immediately springing to mind in this respect is the celebrated 'entrepreneur', the go-ahead businessman on whom Britain, according to the current historical interpretation, built her Empire. Famous examples from the past include Wilkinson and Roebuck in iron and engineering, Minton, Spode, and Wedgwood in pottery, and Peel and Arkwright in textiles. Capacities attributed to them were the willingness to take risks, the ability to turn technological discoveries into commercial products, a talent for organisation, and perfect attunement to the market. In our own century this historically

evolved picture has been enhanced further still by a love of culture and design. Well-known twentieth century examples include Olivetti, Braun, and IBM. This definition of the enlightened entrepreneur also ascribes to him the attributes of a Maecenas. And yet do the great British names answer to this description?

On the basis of research, which as regards the nineteenth century is still in its infancy, there is good reason to assume that many British entrepreneurs enlisted the aid of designers. Leaving aside the legendary Josiah Wedgwood, who has been adequately described elsewhere, it is known, for instance, that Coalbrookdale iron foundry collaborated with French sculptors, with artists from the group centred around Henry Cole (Felix Summerly's Art Manufactures), and with Christopher Dresser. In this industrial area a School of Art was founded in 1853 to provide local companies with well-trained designers. The tile factory of Maw & Co., for example, worked with architects like G.E. Street and William Burges, and with the designer Lewis Day.[6] Christopher Dresser designed between 1862 and 1890 for more than thirty firms at home and abroad. 'As an architect I have as much work as many of my fellows, as an ornamentalist, I have much the largest practice in the United Kingdom . . . there is not a branch of art-manufacture that I do not regularly design patterns for, and I hold regular appointments as 'art advisor' and 'chief designer' to several of our largest art-manufacturing firms.'[7]

All this creates the impression that hiring a pattern-drawer or designer, certainly as far as the more design-sensitive interior objects are concerned, was a widespread practice. However, recurring complaints about the lack of taste and originality of British products indicate rather the reverse. Gillian Naylor describes the problem thus: 'It became increasingly obvious that the French, the Belgians and, to a certain extent, the Prussians, were in the possession of that invisible export known as 'taste' which, it seemed, eluded the majority of British manufacturers and which they would obviously have to acquire in order to become fully competitive.'[8] Fashionable, high-quality goods came mainly from France. British products remained average, as an observant visitor noted on viewing the contents of a

¼ size

THE GREAT EXHIBITION, INDIA SECTION, 1851

LONDON SLUM, ABOUT 1880
as seen by Gustave Doré

PRESENT-DAY SLUM

large store. 'The finer fancy goods are almost exclusively French, but as the lower descriptions are in more daily consumption it brings up the quantity of English to be nearly proportionate.'[9]

When British entrepreneurs choose to work with designers this is generally out of economic interest, just as government interference with design has always been consistently directed at increasing export. When Sir Robert Peel brought up the question of design before Parliament in 1832 and argued for the founding of a National Gallery for the improvement of taste of manufacturers and public alike, he was not acting out of idealism. It so happens that the debate in which he made this suggestion was about the textile export, plagued as it was by foreign competition. In the postwar period the government has made no secret of this either.[10] As for cultural sensibility and design patronage a country such as Italy comes sooner to mind because there, unlike in Britain, there exists a distinct tradition of patronage which has passed on to the industrialists, and which in many cases involves more than just bringing in a designer. At all events, the age when a British entrepreneur gives shape to his social and cultural responsibility through designers or architects has yet to dawn. For where is the British Olivetti, Braun, or IBM?

What of the first part of our definition of an entrepreneur, which comes closer to active enterprise? Towards the end of the nineteenth century this heroic, glorious tradition seemed to be on the wane. Its practitioners, by that time leisure-loving, lazy individuals who had 'made it', lost their alertness and devoted themselves, in keeping with the 'gentleman' image, more to the pursuit of leisure than to their firm. At least this is the intepretation of influential historians like David Landes.[11] In recent years, however, there has been increasing doubt as to the adventurous and efficient nature accredited these heroes of progress. Researchers with their wits about them have come up with quite another picture of the entrepreneur. 'He was an upwardly mobile capitalist, combining a spirit of adventure with rational organisation to minimize risk. He was self-disciplined, abstemious, hard-working, and utilitarian. He lacked culture, sophistication, and any sense of value other than the maximization of profit.'[12] In principle, says P.L. Payne, who wrote a critical appraisal of literature on the entrepreneur, we are dealing with a one-man business whose owner was capitalist, financier, manager, merchant, and salesman all rolled into one, and whose motives in making money lay in the last analysis in acquiring the much-coveted status of gentleman.[13] This brings to mind sooner the capable businessman than the image become legend that I outlined earlier.

For the British entrepreneurs, with raw materials and machines that no-one else had, quite simply monopolised the market. Huge sales both at home and abroad were thus guaranteed. 'Anybody who devotes himself to making money, body and soul,' according to Samuel Smiles, entrepreneur, 'can scarcely fail to make himself rich.'[14] So the risk-taking attribute is open to some doubt. On the basis of their great hopes for the future many entrepreneurs were apparently quite prepared to build up a large firm from scratch – after all, sales success was assured. Perhaps the economic growth and sunny prospects spawned the entrepreneur rather than vice versa.[15]

In this respect, investing in new machines and techniques was more a matter of course than a step in the dark, for it invariably meant an unmistakable improvement in productivity. Payne also reached the conclusion that there were too many entrepreneurs rather than too few. The power of those shining examples still known to us by name, lies according to him in their having had at all times, whatever it took, a monopoly, whether by an agreement between entrepreneur and inventor, or through patents, a specific craft quality, or an original facet of their products.

As for major shortcomings he draws attention to their almost complete ignorance in technical matters and lack of administrative and organisational know-how. Inefficiency and bad management were, at a time when expansion and competition were the order of the day, around 1900, to be the entrepreneur's undoing. An individualist approach no longer worked, concluded sundry government committees during and after the First World War. 'Whilst individualism has been of inestimable advantage in the past, there is reason to fear that individualism by itself may fail to meet the competition of the future in Shipbuilding and Marine Engineering, as

1974 CRISIS

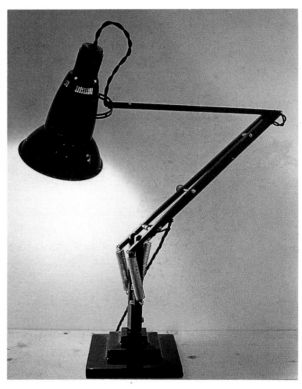

ANGLEPOISE LIGHT, 1934
George Carwardine, Herbert Terry & Sons Ltd., metal,
collection Boymans-van Beuningen Museum, Rotterdam
This desk light, employing the constant-tension jointing principles
found in the human arm, was to become a design classic

it has failed in other industries. We are convinced that the future of the nation depends to a large extent upon increased co-operation in its great industries.'[16] David Landes supplies the coup de grâce by underlining the hamfistedness and complacency characterising British

enterprise. 'Her [Britain's] merchants, who had once seized the markets of the world, took them for granted; the consular reports are full of the incompetence of British exporters, their refusal to suit their goods to the taste and pockets of the client, their unwillingness to try new products in new areas, their insistence that everyone in the world ought to read English and count in pounds, shillings, and pence. Similarly, the British manufacturer was notorious for his indifference to style, his conservatism in the face of new techniques, his reluctance to abandon the individuality of tradition for the conformity implicit in mass production.'[17]

All this seems to strengthen the anti-industrial culture presaged by Wiener and raises the question of whether Great Britain can be described as an enterprising culture at all. The conclusion we are forced to draw from the above sources is that of a series of coincidences, linked to an individualism present at an early stage, a laissez-faire economic policy, and a world monopoly.[18]
The entrepreneur, in the sense of a company owner willing to take risks, possessed with a great talent for organisation, and making and selling innovative products, was more exception than rule.

The workshop in decline

At the beginning of this century the workshop of the world was forced to step down in favour of countries like America and West Germany. Since then its economy has taken a plunge or two, as can be evinced from the literature, distressing to read, on Britain's economic decline, which, over the years, has swelled into a sizable library. For a country with such an illustrious past and used to playing a major role in world affairs this issue seems to have become an obsession. The economic recession, which began in about 1870, has now continued for more than a century.

Whereas in 1870 Britain was still able to account for 32% of world industrial production, this contribution had by 1914 dwindled to 13%.[19] An important cause of this falling back was the persistence of sticking to Free Trade and individualism. Britain lost out on a

BLACK WATCH, 1975
Clive Sinclair, Sinclair Research Ltd., plastics,
collection Boymans-van Beuningen Museum, Rotterdam, gift of mr. W.H. Crouwel
This inexpensive digital timepiece, a sensation in 1975, proved to be
defective in production.

MICROVISION POCKET TELEVISION, 1983
Clive Sinclair, Sinclair Research Ltd., plastics
collection Boymans-van Beuningen Museum, Rotterdam,
gift of Compac
Difficult to obtain, subsequently losing out to the Sony Watchman

second count in its lack of attention to research, standardisation, and specialisation. After 1945 growth of the British economy still lagged far behind that of other Western countries. Whereas the destructive effect of the Second World War led elsewhere in Europe to a firm grasp on industry, and its vigorous modernisation, Britain – affected to a much lesser degree – looked unconcernedly the other way. Modernisation failed to take place. Between 1950 and 1973 Great Britain realised an average annual economic growth of 2.7%, but was being outpaced by its rivals. The industrial productive growth of, say, Japan between 1960 and 1973 was on average 12.6%, that

of America 4.9%, and West Germany 5.5%, as against 3% in Great Britain.[20]

In the seventies, and in particular following the oil crisis of 1973 the downhill trend was furthered by increased competition from low wage countries in the Third World and by the rivalry in terms of quality of America, Japan, and the EEC countries. Many fusions and bankruptcies set in motion a process of de-industrialisation. The traditionally powerful British industries in particular, such as steel, shipbuilding, cars, and machinery, took some hard knocks. The growing inflation also made British industry at this time less

PROTOTYPE LAND-ROVER, 1947
Maurice and Spencer Wilks, The Rover Company

Anthony Sampson, in his study of contemporary Britain cites a few obvious shortcomings: 'antiquated industry; lack of investment; technological backwardness; class divisions and bitter labour relations.'[24] He attributes the postwar economic decline to the fact that the British kept looking back towards the past glory of Empire and the 'heroic' Second World War, and had difficulty accepting their country's new, more mundane role.[25]

It seems that Britain's industrial culture lacks enterprise, to say the least, and that the supposed tradition in this respect is a figment of the imagination. In our century at least, it has been more stifling than stimulating. Another investigation (carried out in 1986) points to the same factors: bad management, not enough investment, a falling behind on the technological front, insufficient education and training, and the inability to turn discoveries into commercial propositions.[26]

C5 ELECTRICALLY POWERED VEHICLE, 1984-85
*Clive Sinclair, Sinclair Vehicles
collection Boymans-van Beuningen Museum, Rotterdam*

competitive. In the year 1986 manufacturing industry accounted for less than 25% of the Gross National Product (GNP) against 40% in Japan and around 32% in countries such as Germany, France, and Italy.[21] We should also note that the steep decline in industrial production between 1979 and 1981 of around 15% has yet to be compensated for. In any case, Britain is still producing less than it did in 1973.[22] David Marquand uses in his penetrating analysis of British politics the analogy of a 'chronic invalid in a snowstorm', and points to two recurring problems. 'British economic agents have repeatedly failed to adapt to the waves of technological and institutional innovation sweeping through the world economy; Britain's political authorities have repeatedly failed to promote more adaptive economic behaviour.'[23] Reactions to the changing economic climate were in his eye defensive rather than preemptive. Also, there were constant complaints about management, trade unions, and education.

MORRIS MINI MINOR, 1959
Alec Issigonis, British Motor Corporation/Morris Motors,
collection the British Motor Industry Heritage Trust
Features such as front-wheel drive, transverse engine, 10-inch wheels
and rubber suspension enabled a car of compact size to be produced
at a modest price

FP PORTABLE COMPUTER, 1985
Sector Design, Apricot
collection Boymans-van Beuningen Museum, Rotterdam

Inventors

Aside from the decline of the traditionally strong bread-and-butter industries – cars, domestic appliances, office furniture, machine tools – this last-named aspect, how to deal with inventions, is quite a problem. In research and development the British are exceptionally

capable in some fields, such as aircraft, weapons, nuclear power stations, computers, and engines. Flourishing industries in the British economy are currently the electronics and pharmaceutical industries and biotechnology. There also seem to be enough examples of individual pioneers of genius who startled the world with innovative, intelligent products to justify speaking of a tradition. British design classics include the *Anglepoise* lamp (1934) designed by G. Carwardine for Herbert Terry & Sons; the successful, compact *Mini Minor* automobile (1959) by the engineer Alex Issigonis with its engine placed crosswise; the miniature bicycle by Alec Moulton (1964); the compact computers and digital watch by Clive Sinclair in the seventies and eighties. More recent examples include James Dyson, an interior designer who improved the vacuum cleaner and designed an ingenious wheelbarrow, as well as a multi-purpose military boat;

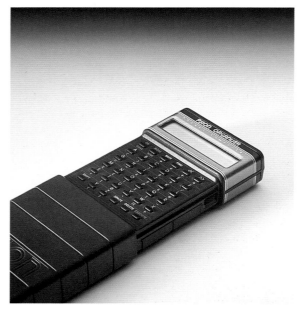

ORGANISER COMPUTER, 1985
Stephen Frazer, Psion, ABS
collection Boymans-van Beuningen Museum, Rotterdam

Roger Dee, self-taught and brought up on a farm, who constructed a small motor-driven tip-cart; the surgeon David Sharpe with a disposable means of keeping wounds open; song writer Stephen Randall with an electronic guitar synthesizer. Sinclair, Moulton, and Dyson are the most famous of these, founding one or more firms on the strength of their findings.

Clive Sinclair, who in 1972 brought out the first low-priced calculator (the *Executive*), was, however, soon left behind by the Japanese. His inexpensive digital timepiece, the *Black Watch*, a sensation in 1975, proved to be defective in production. Sinclair's revolutionary, compact, and once again very cheap home computers suffered from the enormous demand far outpacing the supply, and later from competition. The *Microvision* pocket TV was difficult to obtain, subsequently losing out to the Sony *Watchman*. Finally, his electrically powered vehicle, the *C5*, with a weak engine and low capacity, turned out a disaster. Sinclair's ideas for products are brilliant, but his technology, marketing, and production techniques fall short of the mark. The same goes for Alex Moulton. James Dyson came to grief with his vacuum cleaner in both production and distribution. Nobody wanted to make it in Britain. The Rotork *Sea Truck*, for which he went to work for Rotork in the seventies, had to sell abroad first before the British government would have anything to do with it. It is Dyson's opinion that the British market has no appetite for competition. There is no need for firms to vie with one another, as the home market has already resolved into a few big names in each sector.[27] A low price is their only weapon against, say, Japan.

Complaints about the dearth of adventurous entrepreneurs of vision are legion. Reports and case studies repeatedly underline the fact that Britain has little idea of how to sell or market her inventions. Replying to this, Mrs. Thatcher recently put it as follows: 'First we did the research . . . only to see the ideas from our research suddenly redesigned and repackaged by others who perhaps gave more attention to their markets . . . we did the work and they made the profits.'[28] Privatisation is one of her weapons. Powerful, private companies are to lead to a more effectively functioning market.

MOULTON BICYCLE, 1964
Alex Moulton, Moulton Bicycles
The suspension system allows for small wheels, which are tougher and lighter than conventional wheels and cut down on inertia, which makes pedalling easier

In addition, an interest in designing, marketing, and management is being vigorously stimulated through the Enterprise Initiative of the Department of Trade and Industry. In 1987 the Confederation of British Industry, in the wake of a seminar on industrial design in Downing Street, launched a campaign to 'improve the design of new products as a means of boosting Britain's export and creating new jobs.'[29] New and well-designed products are to contribute to a more competitive position in world industry.

The new 'enterprise culture' has found a willing ear amongst those companies who have since opened their doors to a younger generation, to whom professionalism has more appeal than the amateur. The enterprise culture propagated by the government seems to be bearing fruit, judging by the proliferation of small new High-Tech companies and by modernised production technologies, sometimes to an extreme degree. Whether this will result in a healthier attitude to innovation as a process, and the successful introduction of new discoveries onto the market, remains to be seen. For the time being, inherited hierarchical structures, individualism, and the inability to react quickly to problems remain a stumbling block. According to Gordon Edge, chief group executive of PA Technology: ' . . . in this country we are still proccupied with the inventor rather than the process of innovation. We are too concerned with the creation of technological heroes, who simply cannot live up to expectations. When they fall, they bring in their wake yet more disillusioned investors, who blame the problems on technology itself, rather than on their own foolishness in thinking that a Whittle or Brunel can be born with equal effect into the broad technological sophistication of today.'[30] An absence of background, structure, and

tradition are still obstacles to interdisciplinary teamwork on a high professional level, through which designer-entrepreneurs and inventors seem to me to be more at home amongst eccentric amateurs and 'one-hit wonders'. They are proof that the individualism dominating Britain is both its strength and its weakness.

BICYCLE WHEEL, PROTOTYPE, 1984
Seymour & Powell, General Electric Plastics
The 35cc two-stroke engine and petrol tank is integrated with the wheel

CYCLON VACUUMCLEANER
designed in 1979 by James Dyson,
produced in 1985 by Apex Inc., Japan,
collection James Dyson, Bath

chapter four   **DESIGN AS A COMMODITY**

Contrasting sharply with the anti-industrial culture is the rapid rise of a multitude of giant design consultancies. In the last decade design has emerged as a professional and extremely profitable branch of industry. Compared to the fifties there has been a revolutionary about-turn within the profession. Looking back on that decade Wally Olins characterises design in the fifties as 'quaint, somewhat precious and only of peripheral significance to the real world.'[1]

The atmosphere then pervading the profession was individualistic and convivial – rather like a gentlemen's club. Any self-evident integration with industry was for the time being to remain very much wishful thinking. Thirty years later this amateurish set-up has become transformed as if by magic into a picture of vast multi-disciplinary design consultancies who with a constant stream of products, images, and styles are saturating the environment with 'design'. With a staff exceeding 200, clients throughout the world, and a Stock Exchange listing they represent an economic power not to be underestimated. In 1985 they together managed a turnover of a staggering 990 million pounds.[2] The era when industrial design was a religion for the initiated seems to be well and truly behind us. Design in the eighties means big business, and is now a household word. Instead of isolation, lofty ideals, and

the fight for recognition it now stands for glamour, luxury, and status. What do these giant offices do, and how can we explain their spectacular rise to success?

The majority of consultancies are multi-disciplinary, in other words operating in all markets. 'A hunger for versatility and the drive to extend range are discernible among consultancies of every size and type'.[3] They offer a broad spectrum of services ranging from rough drafts to marketing. A good example of such a comprehensive approach is PA. Beginning life as a management consultancy it spawned around 1968 PA Technology, an office geared to the commercial application of new technological discoveries such as the microchip. From there it then saw possibilities for expansion in the exterior of the product, which led to the foundation in 1975 of a third division, PA Design. Their first joint commission was for hi-fi equipment. PA Design's client list continues to reflect the link with technological innovation, revealing a distinct concentration on consumer goods, and electronic, medical, and communications equipment. Two years ago PA Design was swallowed up by the Michael Peters Group, a large design office and in 1983 one of the first to be launched on the Stock Exchange.[4] By acquiring Brand New, specialists in marketing, PA Design completes the picture of an

POWDER BOX WITH FESTIVAL OF BRITAIN LOGO
designed in 1951 by Abram Games
collection Boymans-van Beuningen Museum, Rotterdam
British design in the fifties: optimistic, amateurish, anecdotal

JUG AND MUG, 1930
Keith Murray, Josiah Wedgwood & sons Ltd., earthenware
collection Boymans-van Beuningen Museum, Rotterdam
A promise of the collaboration of industries with designers from the thirties

POSTER, 1932
Edward McKnight Kauffer

integrated consultancy that looks after its products from concept to market.

The pamphlets of Fitch & Co., too, give rise in their imposing variety of available services to a growing astonishment. These include shopping centres, amusement parks, and airports: 'We shoulder the heaviest tasks, from mass seating, catering and lighting, through customised fixtures, to the installing of complex telecommunications systems.'[5] Against these can be weighed the smaller firms such as Seymour & Powell, started as a two-man enterprise and specialising rather than diversifying. It focuses on style and the 'look' of consumer goods and, when necessary, recruits outside expertise. The fields that generally predominate, however, are corporate identity, printed matter, packaging, shops, exhibitions, and interiors – matters involving graphic design and presentation.

From a report by the Design Council it appears that this growth is of a recent date.[6] More than half all consultancies saw the light of day in the eighties. Already a quarter have more than 100 employees. In this respect Fitch & Co., with a staff of more than 360, including 220 designers, carries off the laurels. From this it transpires too that the giant concerns predominate with almost half the market in their possession. We are talking here about vast sums of money. Between 1980 and 1985 turnovers doubled and profits trebled, increases which are expected to continue in the foreseeable future. And that has to be so, for a listing on the Stock Exchange requires a growth in profits of more than 20% per year. This diversification is one way to achieve growth and an increase in profits. In these cases the business of making money is priority number one and practices seem more geared to profit than to anything else. Consequently design has burgeoned into a considerable economic factor in the services sector.

An ever-increasing share of these profits stems from foreign clients looking for a British 'finishing touch' to their goods, interiors, and retail-outlets. Pentagram, for example, has branches in New York and San Francisco, while its commissions in Japan increase daily. Minale, Tattersfield & Partners operate from Cologne, London, Madrid, and Milan. PA Design has design groups in London, Paris, Melbourne, and Sydney. Fitch & Co. saw the foreign share of their turnover increase from 10-15% in 1987 to 25% in 1988.[7] The above-mentioned report predicts for 1992 a design export worth no less than one billion pounds. Business is indeed booming.

Can Britain make it?

The rise of the giant design consultancies seems paradoxical if we look at the history of British product design, which cannot boast a great tradition of industries collaborating with designers, though the thirties brought promising steps in that direction. Concerns like Wedgwood and Stevens & Williams worked with Eric Ravilious and Keith Murray, amongst others, while Frank Pick pursued with London Underground Railway a policy of a progressiveness hitherto unheard of. There were, besides, firms like PEL (tubular steel furniture), E.K. Cole (radios), and Edinburgh Weavers (textiles) who now and again hired a designer. Gordon Russell, Jack Pritchard, and Wells Coates manufactured their creations themselves.

Though the idea of 'good' mass production began to appeal to designers like Jack Howe, Douglas Scott, and the young Kenneth Grange the good-natured, somewhat amateurish atmosphere changed

little during the fifties. Integration with industry was making slow progress. 'Within industry, and even within those companies which have used industrial designers with apparent success, the term must usually be spoken gently at the end of a technological discourse if it is to escape argument and mockery', to quote Bruce Archer who in 1954 drew attention to 'scepticism and hostility in Britain towards industrial design.'[8] Herbert Read complained that 'our design in almost every industry is forty to fifty years out-of-date.'[9] In point of fact, Kenneth Grange was one of the few all-round product designers in postwar Britain, despite the more scientific approach to the profession propagated by the CoID (Council of Industrial Design), and the rapprochement of engineer and designer.

Dissatisfaction with manufacturers lacking vision remained the overriding sentiment. 'Only a few manufacturers know how to go about getting an industrial designer, or even know that trained designers exist to help them', declared *Design* in 1966.[10] Even Gordon Russell, for years director of the CoID, was forced to conclude

STACKING CHAIR, 1962
Robin Day, Hille, polypropylene
The most successful modern British chair

CORPORATE IDENTITY FOR REUTERS, 1973
Alan Fletcher of Pentagram

around 1980 that the attitude of British industry towards designers was no better than it had been in 1945.[11]

The rise of the consultant

And yet the consultant does not appear to be that recent a phenomenon. A precedent, and quite a rarity in its day, was the Design Research Unit (DRU), the first large-scale multi-disciplinary design practice, founded in 1943 on the hopes for a new world. The designers Milner Gray, Misha Black, and Norbert Dutton, the architects Frederick Gibberd and Sadie Speight, and the engineer Felix Samuely joined forces under the directorship of Herbert Read and Marcus Brumwell. 'The function of DRU is to focus on every project it undertakes the combined knowledge and experience of several creative minds since it believes that only by pooling the talents of a team of designers is it possible to offer a service capable of meeting every demand from the wide and varied field of present-day activity.'[12] Team work, research, and a rational approach were the mainstays with which to give shape to this new world. The offer of a complete service announced in its brochure seems somewhat bombastic, yet was made good by way of exceptionally large commissions such as their share in the exhibitions Britain Can Make It (1946) and the Festival of Britain (1951), interiors for the SS Oriana (1956) and locomotives, and corporate identity for British Rail (from 1956). DRU dominated Britain's design world, most evidently in the field of exhibitions, corporate identity, and engineering.

Competition, however, was not to be ruled out. Ogle Design (1954), Conran (1955), and Allied Industrial Designers (1959) made their appearance on the design stage. From within the ranks of the Society of Industrial Artists (SIA), the professional society, there emerged a group of consultants, in doing so raising the question of professional recognition. 'The position of the general consultant designer is a comparatively new one in this country . . . Under the very different conditions that exist over here [compared to America

MATCHES PACKAGING FOR ASDA STORES, 1987
John Lloyd, Margaret Nolan of Lloyd Northover,
and illustrator Andrew Gibb
From a matchbook to a motor body

where consultants had already existed in the thirties] there has been a tendency to view the general consultant as a kind of design department 'trouble shooter', flitting from one industry to the next.'[13] It was evidently a matter of getting used to this voracious breed of designer, defined by the SIA as one with his own practice or attached to an independent office, and operating in a number of fields. Bruce Archer was one who wondered whether such an all-rounder

could exist. 'If a body of general consultant designers, in the sense of design policy makers, is to grow up in Britain, designers will have to demonstrate that they are competent in the broader skills of marketing and brand imagery, as well as in the finer points of the specific design fields which they profess to serve directly.'[14]
These were prophetic words, that in the coming twenty-five years would be borne out with a vengeance.

In 1963 the General Consultant Designers' Group of the SIA included twenty-one members claiming to be able to design everything 'from a matchbook to a motor body' whether or not with

LOGO FOR DUTCH SUPERMARKET CHAIN ALBERT HEIJN, 1965
James Pilditch and John Harris of AID
British consultancies made tracks for foreign climes

outside help.[15] In their case the systematic and mathematical design approach so much relished by the CoID was conspicuous by its absence. Their growth was a very gradual affair owing much more to a commercially aggressive attitude. The practices kept coming: Fletcher, Forbes & Gill, later Pentagram, (1962-63), Wolff Olins (1965), OMK (1966), BIB (1967), and Moggridge Associates (1969). The acceptance of corporate identity and the rising popularity of design in the exuberant, consumer-orientated sixties gave them self-confidence. 'British designers began to realise that they had flair and wit, that they had the discipline of the Europeans and the commercial instincts of the Americans . . .'[16] Besides the popular design the emphasis lay at that time on design management. In this combination of the fashionable and businesslike was laid the basis for the strength of British design in the eighties.

Using their newly-acquired self-confidence as a springboard the first consultancies made tracks for foreign climes; AID to the Netherlands in 1964 with a commission for corporate identity for the Albert Heijn supermarket chain, and Wolff Olins to West Germany and America because this firm saw a gap in the foreign market its particular qualities could fill. The result was commissions for worldwide corporate identity for Renault and Volkswagen-Audi. The growth of multi-disciplinary design offices continued steadily, as a commercial stream that seemed to operate outside Pop and the Design Council. In 1972 Pentagram effected a fusion of product and graphic design; Rodney Fitch of the Conran Design Group decided to set up his own practice; and PA Design was born of PA Technology. Offices averaged a staff of fifty and did much work for industries made design-conscious by stiff competition such as transport, the financial service-industries, wines and spirits, and, especially, the retail trade.

After the crisis of 1973 the tendency to specialise and contract out took an upward trend amongst industries, who were switching over more and more to the recruitment of outside consultants. For this the growing influence of marketing and the professionalism of American firms and designers were also to blame. The recession for one was driving British designers en masse to foreign shores,

MARCELLO
MINALE

BRIAN
TATTERSFIELD

ADVERTISEMENT, 1986
Lucy Walker of Minale Tattersfield and Partners,
Design and advertising merge into one another

particularly to the Middle East, France, and America. 'It is beginning to be acknowledged that British and not Italian design is more quintessentially European', as *Design* pointed out, not without pride, nor without some concern about the import of these goods foreign-made yet of British origin.[17] Wolff Olins, AID, and Conran earned half of their 1976 turnover outside Britain. By that time AID had offices in Norway, Brussels, Stockholm, and Zurich, with Frankfurt in the offing. Thus the arrival and expansion of design consultancies were already a fact prior to the eighties.

This aspect of British design was not, however, given a place in design history, as the above growth was largely founded on graphic work, which most handbooks treated as beyond their scope; nor was there, unfortunately, a general work on the subject. Besides, much work belonged to the 'invisibles' such as interiors and architecture.[18] The many commissions from abroad kept the consultancies from the British design scene, while their commercial approach produced standardised designs rather than design landmarks. Only when these offices began to exhibit an unmistakable power within the British economy and their work began popping up on every street corner (particularly in the many 'designed' shop interiors) was their existence no longer possible to ignore.

The Britishness of the British design consultancies

How are we to explain the tremendous prosperity of these consultancies, leaving aside the tendency already observed earlier to contract out, specialisation, and the importance of marketing? What did the British consultancies have that the others lacked? British designers were quick to look beyond the UK to the foreign market, not least because British firms were not producing much at that time and had little interest in working with a designer. In addition, education was turning out more designers than the country could absorb. These pragmatic considerations aside, they do seem, judging from the response they elicited, to have had something to offer. Of overriding importance was their reputation in the graphic

CORDLESS KETTLE, 1985
Seymour & Powell, Tefal SA, France
kemetal, polypropylene

field, particularly in corporate identity. In addition they appear, however, to have possessed other much sought-after capacities. 'It is readily agreed that, as far as Europe is concerned, British design consultants are the greatest exponents of design as a tool for solving management and marketing problems. Nowhere else can companies find the multi-disciplinary approach favoured by the larger groups.'[19] Already in the seventies the prevailing approach was forcefully commercial and professional, laying great stress on designing as a strategy, and on marketing. Evidently there were few foreign consultancies able to offer such a wide array of services. In a country like West Germany, for instance, the tradition of the industrial designer on the payroll has been long established. Then again, Italian design is rooted in small companies and the personality cult of the *maestro* – the designer as *prima donna*. Owing to their broad technical background British designers were moreover in a position to advise on matters of production technique, something that their American colleagues, for example, since Raymond Loewy's day geared to styling, were incapable of doing. There this aspect was often contracted out to non-designers. The education of British designers, with great attention paid to engineering, was therefore of a relatively high standard too. A further advantage added in the seventies was that British design talent was relatively cheap owing to the devalued pound. Martin Roberts of the Conran Design Group adds: 'British designers have a reputation for getting things done on time and at a reasonable price.'[20] The pragmatic, practical, fair-minded British designer – heedful of the British tradition, willing to compromise – had found with his in no way extreme or outspoken design tradition, an effective way of meeting the demand by the international market for elegant, acceptable products.

Decisive in the last few years, however, has been the pressure of a market with an increasingly international character and the competition of Japan and others, because of which firms have had to keep stepping up the fight for their share of the market. The rapid upsurge of the land of the rising yen – the result of bold investments in new technologies and a keen sense of style and needs – proves that the priority accorded the low price is by no means always well-

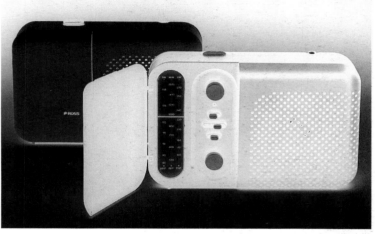

RADIO, 1985
Graham Thomson of PA Design (now Brand New Ltd.),
Ross Electronics, ABS

placed. Moreover electronics, or rather the microchip, has shifted the attention away from the interior to the exterior. The technology is for most products universal and scarcely open to improvement. Differentiation, specialisation, and quality are the new magic words necessary for a product to succeed with the consumer. And what other word fits in with these better than 'design'?

The government: design or decline

The British government, too, is waking up to the potential of design. John Butcher, until recently responsible for design at the Department of Trade and Industry, has finally understood the message transmitted for years by the Design Council and other champions of design. 'Design is one of the major factors influencing the market

ERGO HIP FLASK, 1986
Chris Middleton, Troika Ltd., pewter
Expensive gadgets for the trendy 'design' consumer

success of British products, and an essential key to the country's economic revival. Now, more than ever, firms must respond to the demands of the market place.'[21] Prime Minister Thatcher has also grasped in her own energetic way this particular bull by the horns. From 1982 onwards her government has been pumping money into stimulating design by way of the so-called Funded Consultancy

Scheme (later renamed Enterprise Initiative).

This meant that firms with 60 to 100 employees would have the cost of fifteen days' design consultancy reimbursed in full followed by another fifteen days at half the price. In the first two years the government spent something like 10 million pounds on this scheme, rising to a total of 25 million pounds in 1987.[22] Up to and including May 1984 it sustained 1500 projects in this way. It also organises seminars on design and supports a Design Management Unit at the London Business School. Advice on marketing, technology, and management is subsidised via the Enterprise Initiative of the Department of Trade and Industry. The government expects costs up till 1991 to total 250 million pounds.[23] These measures, by no means to be scoffed at, and launched with the conviction characterising this government, were adopted to ensure that design became a matter of national importance, and they contributed to the dramatic upsurge of consultancies.

About the motives behind all this the government itself leaves no room for doubt. 'The main priority at the moment is to increase the competitiveness of British products, both at home and abroad.'[24] Design is the tonic for Britain's ailing economy and must resuscitate industry by way of stiff competition. And yet where are these British products the government refers to? The blossoming of the large consultancies points more to the growth of design as a service industry, design as an export as software rather than hardware. What the government gives with one hand, moreover, it takes back with the other. And can the expected boom in employment and production cancel out the damage done by the cuts the government has inflicted on industry?

Commercial art

Basic to the rise and success of the giant consultancies is to my mind, however, the graphic tradition in British design. In this field are to be found the roots of the professionalising of design in Britain. For example, the members of the first Society of Industrial Artists,

CHEF KITCHEN MACHINE, 1960
*Kenneth Grange of Pentagram, Kenwood Ltd., die cast metal, plastic,
collection Pentagram, London
The British Braun, and successful example of designer and
industry working together professionally*

INPUTS RANGE, 1972
Conran Associates, Airfix Plastics, ABS
British designers have a reputation for getting things done
on time and at a reasonable price

the professional society founded in 1930, were mainly illustrators and poster designers. In those days they called themselved commercial artists and were the first to integrate with industry. Usually this was by way of advertising agencies, which either bought up designers or comissioned them in a free-lance capacity. Large agencies of the thirties include Stuarts, Crawfords, J. Walter Thompson, and the London Press Exchange. Advertising magazines like *Penrose Annual* and *Commercial Art* were for designers the most important way of keeping abreast of international developments. Such firms as Shell-Mex, British Petrol, and Imperial Airways raised poster design to a high level by bringing in reputable designers like James Gardner, Ashley Havinden, Hans Schleger, and Edward McKnight Kauffer.[25] The last two were emigrants, as were F.H.K. Henrion, Lewis Woudhuysen, and Ernest Hoch. They brought with them to Britain, according to teacher and designer Robin Kinross, a different

approach to design: 'These people were among the leading figures in the development of graphic design out from its small, drawing-board concerns and on to the new terrain of corporate work.'[26] Emigrants were also to play a vital role in the growth of Britain's reputation in the field of exhibition design and display. Besides the renowned but craft-based typographers and printers who since Morris' time had swelled into a powerful group, a commercial graphic trend was clearly taking shape. The driving force behind, and springboard for, professionalising design further was the talent for presenting and selling goods, services, and corporate identity.

During the Second World War the Ministry of Information, founded in 1939, took over under the inspiring leadership of Frank Pick the role of the stimulating client. With the graphic designer Milner Gray as head of the exhibition design department it became a rich source of talent spawning in 1943 the large consultancy DRU. DRU united industrial and graphic design and architecture, and was another to excel in exhibition commissions and graphic work, in

FLEXY AQUA 3, 1987
Jeff Martin, Chris Murray of Brand New Ltd.,
Holt-Lloyd Ltd., polypropylene

CORPORATE IDENTITY FOR ARAL, 1975
Wolff Olins

CORPORATE IDENTITY FOR Q8, 1986
Wolff Olins

particular corporate identity schemes. It was graphic designers who set up the first group practices too. During the fifties most consultancies neglected product design in favour of the more profitable graphic commissions including much packaging and corporate identity.

Connections with the world of advertising remained healthy. Until well into the sixties firms would probe their advertising agencies for advice on a variety of commercial matters. The larger agencies had their own staff of packaging designers and only at the

end of the seventies did professional designers pose a serious threat. They often functioned as patron to designers and photographers. Of great significance is the alliance of the two professions in the Designers and Art Directors Association (D&AD) founded in 1962. Publicity agent and designer in Britain share the same background in terms of education. Wally Olins of Wolff Olins comes from the advertising world, as do Bob Gill of Pentagram and Marcello Minale and Brian Tattersfield. The dividing line between the two is vague: they merge into one another. Corporate identity and image overlap

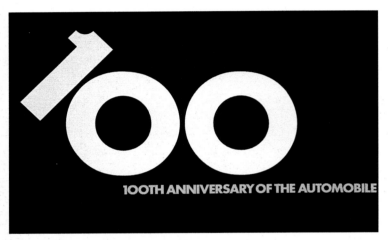

POSTER TO COMMEMORATE THE 100TH ANNIVERSARY
OF THE BIRTH OF THE DAIMLER-BENZ CAR, 1985
Alan Fletcher of Pentagram

the world's 'foremost global know-how company.'[29] In 1988 they too bought up a design consultancy based in London and California, with prospective branches in Italy, Germany, Switzerland, Austria, and Scandinavia. National boundaries become blurred and the large-scale seems to win every time, with money the great generator, in a branch of industry that knows no limits. Then again, the working method and approach to design adopted by the consultancies is now no different to that of the advertising agencies. Brian Boylan, managing director of Wolff Olins explains: 'the designer Michael Wolff realised the power of visual expression and impression. The advertising man Wally Olins brought a businesslike approach in, the power of the application.'[30] And last but by no means least, the character of the design process is nothing like it was. There has been a slow but steady shift from the durable, rational, and technical to the short-lived, fashionable, and easy to sell. In the following chapter, which deals with the retail boom – an occurrence crucial to these developments – I will go into this at greater length.

as regards content too. Further, the many packaging commissions clearly turned graphic designers into salesmen. According to Robin Kinross advertising dominated to such a degree as to elicit at the end of the sixties a reaction from the more socially aware designers, who then rejected the consumer society.[27] Seen in retrospect this rejection was merely fleeting, for in the eighties the advertising and design worlds are once again hand in glove; almost, one could say, as never before.

Advertising agencies take over design consultancies, and vice versa in 1986 WCRS (Wright Collins Rutherford Scott) bought up two consultancies within a few months; a year later holding company WPP (Wire and Plastics Products) absorbed its sixth design practice.[28] Design offices are becoming increasingly active in the fields of marketing and management; as to this their brochures leave no room for doubt. The Saatchi brothers want their firm to function like a supermarket where big concerns can come for all sorts of advice,

PENCIL SHARPENER, 1987
*Kenneth Grange of Pentagram,
Oun International Ltd., Japan, die cast zinc alloy,
collection Pentagram, London*

DESIGNED BY PELIKAN
FOR THE OUN COLLECTION

chapter five   **A NATION OF SHOPKEEPERS**

At no other time in history could the description 'a nation of shopkeepers' by Napoleon be better applied to Britain than today, with the shops becoming more and more like museums, and the museums like shops. The cause? In a word, 'design'. According to *The Economist* four out of the top ten European retailers are British.[1] It is as if the British had discovered a new way of shopping and were feverishly engaged in exporting it worldwide. Inasmuch as their chain stores (Habitat, Laura Ashley, Body Shop, Mothercare, Tie Rack, and so on) have yet to become firmly established on the Continent there is an army of designers all set to Anglicise the shops of Europe – the Conran Design Group with Prisunic in France; AID with the Belgian supermarkets Priba and Delhaize de Lion; and, more recently, Fitch and David Davies Associates with the department store De Bijenkorf and Mexx fashion house in the Netherlands. Not to mention the racks of goods in British wrappings, able to impart to the most wretched of foodstuffs an air of haute cuisine. In the eighties a flood of new shops and shop interiors altered drastically the look of London's streets. It made design front-page news and contributed to the rapid growth of the giant design consultancies. What is it, then, that makes the British, rather than any other nation, so good in this field? Why does London set the pace here, and what does this development tell us of the British designer?

High Street free-for-all

A curious phenomenon to be met with in Britain is that every High Street looks the same. Whether it be Boots, Marks & Spencer, Sainsbury's, W.H. Smith, Habitat, Dixon's, Mothercare, Tesco, Next, Joseph, or Body Shop all branches of a particular concern are as peas in a pod. The chain store dominates the British retail trade as in no other country. In the United Kingdom the ten largest shopping chains together control 65% of the market.

In West Germany, for example, this is 26%, whereas the independent shops there control 45%.[2] This tendency towards the large-scale got underway in 1955, gaining momentum in the sixties. The drive towards greater efficiency and concentration forced the small, independent shopkeepers off the market in favour of the chain and multiple stores, whose share of the market rose between 1961 and 1970 from 28% to 36.8%.[3] They vied not only with one another, but constituted a threat to the department stores who in the seventies balefully watched their own share drop. Furthermore there was considerable overlapping in what shops had to offer, and to whom. And finally, high rents and the lack of space in the inner city turned the High Street into one big commercial battlefield.

To begin with, each chain store adopted a recognisable corporate identity so as to be distinguishable from the rest and to underline its individuality. In 1956 *Design* magazine gave as examples Liberty's, Simpson's, Harvey Nichols, D.H. Evans, and John Lewis. Apart from window displays little attention was being paid as yet to interiors. And while the rising prosperity of the sixties led to a refining of the articles on sale, keeping the price down remained a crucial factor in winning over customers. The increase in self-service shifted the accent to the packaging, which had to catch the eye. Sainsbury's supermarket chain is a well-known example of those days of a concern pursuing a consistent design policy based on its own brand of goods. Marks & Spencer was another with a long-standing corporate identity based on its own products.

Since recently, however, the battle is no longer confined to packaging, advertising, corporate identity, and a lower price, but has on the whole shifted to atmosphere, style, quality, and target group. Inviting, refined shop interiors and concepts created by the large design consultancies vie with one another in their powers to entice. These have become important weapons in a competitive struggle getting more formidable by the day.

The Conran effect

The most important pace-setter in this move to refine further and bring more 'design' to Britain's High Streets was Terence Conran. His Habitat shop concept breathed fresh life into the retail trade of the sixties. The strength of Habitat lay not just in its offer of a complete style of living, but, much more than that, on its being geared to a younger public. The first Habitat shop, opened in 1964, had this in common with the boutiques popping up everywhere at that time. The young – hitherto ignored on all sides – were now able

to enjoy modern life, at not too great a cost. This constituted a crucial breakthrough for modern taste, until then glaringly conspicuous in most British shops by its absence, certainly as far as furniture was concerned. Modern design with the young as target group was a newly-discovered gap in the market.

Conran's shop for switched-on people, where the staff dressed in Quant and were coiffured by Sassoon, expanded into an empire with shops all over the world and an annual turnover in 1983 of

CORPORATE IDENTITY FOR GALT TOYS, 1962
Ken Garland Associates

JIGSA S

In putting together jigsaws children learn to distinguish shapes and patterns – a most useful skill when learning, later, to read.
At first jigsaws are used like fitting toys, the 2 year old repeats them over and over again, enjoying success in finding the right piece for the right space. Nearly all young children enjoy simple jigsaws if given at the right age. Start with the simplest 5 to 6 pieces, then gradually progress to more and more pieces.

THIRD + FO RTH YEARS

The heyday for toys. At this age curiosity knows no bounds. Every type of suitable toy should be made available to the child, for trying out, experimenting and learning, for discovering his own particular aptitudes. Bricks and jigsaws and constructional toys; painting and scribbling and making things; sand and water play; toys for imaginative and pretending play; the first social games for learning to play and get on with others.

Watch children of this age at play, how concentrated and serious they are – and rightly so, for play to them is a serious business, it is work, it is learning about the world and growing up.

FIRST THREE EARS

Don't underestimate a baby's ability to profit from the right play materials; things to grasp, feeling different textures and weights; things to listen to, rattles, squeakers, bells; things to watch, mobiles, balloons.

The more that is discovered about our early development, the more apparent it becomes that these very first years are the most important of all in establishing an ability for learning. It is worth remembering that one of the most difficult tasks of our lives, learning a language, takes place in these years.

380 million.[4] The entire lack of competition in Britain in this field can be blamed on this expansion.[5] This combination of quality at a low price with a young target group Conran applied to other areas in similar need such as restaurants (the Soup Kitchens, 1954); clothing, toys, and other articles for children (Mothercare, 1981); furniture for the post-Habitat generation (Heal & Son, 1983); fashion (Hepworth, 1982; Now, and Richard Shops in 1983); British Home Stores, and so on. Here, too, the chain store and the large-scale were the order of the day. Meanwhile the existing shops, especially those selling fashion and department stores, realised that they could not simply sit back and do nothing. For them Conran's success, which proved that 'design' could be big business, was one of the incentives to introduce change.[6]

The Conran effect made itself felt in the British design world in other ways too. For Conran's career reflects a general tendency towards vertical expansion. Besides the above-named restaurants and shops there were the Conran Design Group, founded in 1955; Elektra Risk Capital set up in 1981; the Conran Roche office for architecture and urban planning (1982); the Design Museum at Butler's Wharf (formerly the Boilerhouse) sponsored by Conran from 1981; and the publishers Conran Octopus (1983). From a textile designer Terence Conran changed into a go-ahead businessman, a sort of Robert Maxwell of British design. Other design practices adopted this broad approach also. They became more and more like business conglomerates operating on every level. Fitch, for instance, is active in the retail trade as the Fitch Benoy Shopping Centre Consortium, which besides Fitch & Co Design Consultants comprises the Fitch Benoy architects' office and SRU (Specialist Research Unit) for research into consumer shopping behaviour.

Finally the Conran Design Group has exerted a tremendous influence on the British High Street. This office designed not only all Habitat branches, but in the process became involved with Gatwick Airport, Miss Selfridge, Marks & Spencer, and the fashion chain stores Top Shop and Wallis. Apart from the direct influence of the

above on other shops who were modernised and given a new interior, there was another major, indirect influence. It is a remarkable fact that the foremost shop designers of today, like Rodney Fitch and David Davies, learned the ropes of their profession as members of the Conran Design Group. While working there Fitch was responsible for the successful design in 1970 of the Top Shop fashion house. Within sixteen weeks this gave an increase in turnover of 50%, and nine years later Top Shop had blossomed into a chain of 90 shops.[7] In 1971, after the vicissitudes surrounding the ill-starred Conran-Ryman fusion, Fitch bought up the Conran Design Group, two years later renaming it Fitch & Co. Conran's own design office was henceforth known as Conran Associates. David Davies was another to work at Conran's, as a graphic designer and art director, until he, too, formed his own consultancy in 1982. With clients like Tesco, Marks & Spencer, and Next, David Davies Associates (DDA) is likewise specialised in shops.

The boutique as cocktail party

Besides competition and the successful example of Conran, of great influence on the look of Britain's High Streets were the boutiques of the sixties. First in line was Mary Quant in 1955 with her Bazaar, followed by John Michael in 1957 and John Stephen, who in 1959 rented his first shop in Carnaby Street. Within ten days Bazaar was sold out; by 1956 Michael was the owner of seventeen branches, by which time Stephen had ten boutiques in Carnaby Street.[8] Barbara Hulanicki's Biba began life as a mail order company. Her first dress, advertised in the Daily Mirror at 15 pounds, elicited 6000 orders! In 1964 she opened her first shop. The revolutionary London Look, aimed at the young, filled a gap in the market. '. . .the need was so strong, we couldn't fail', explained Quant.[9] Swinging London had become a reality.

As I see it London's boutiques paved the way for the eighties situation because – in their attention to packaging, interiors, and graphic design – they raised 'design' as a whole to a key commercial

PACKAGING FOR BSC, 1969
Hans Schleger & Associates

Other concerns – Top Shop, Wallis, Etam, and Burton's come to mind – set up specialist chains aimed at a young target group. The boutiques pointed the way to the specialisation of the seventies and eighties. For instance, Biba's second and third shops were laid out like supermarkets; were these, then, the first lifestyle mini-stores?

Thus the British boutiques spearheaded general trends in shopping, not only that of specialisation – in terms of product, taste, or target group – but many others besides, all treated today as standard practice. For were the boutiques of the sixties not putting into practice then what would be propagated en masse by the shopping gurus of today and tomorrow? By this I mean individualism, and shopping as entertainment. 'Shopping is fun', insisted the boutique proprietors twenty years back. Mary Quant spoke of 'a sort of permanently running cocktail party', and there was indeed entertainment aplenty in the small, bizarrely designed interiors.[10] Finally, by producing small numbers of articles quickly, the boutiques acquired a structure that was extremely flexible – a practice now resorted to generally by shopkeepers.

Design fever

Once the economic crisis of the mid-seventies had cast its shadow over the euphoria of mass consumption the cocktail party was over. The boutiques vanished and the department stores are reported to have become lifeless. *Design* complained in 1977 of conservative management in the retail trade with no feeling for the customer, and described shop interiors as dull.[11] All was quiet once more in Britain's High Streets. But not, I should add, for long. The harbingers of a new hedonism were already in evidence.

In 1973 Conran opened a shop in Brompton Road, an area that fifteen years later as Brompton Cross would have the greatest 'design' shop density in London. In 1975 punk made its first appearance in London. Thanks to designers like Vivienne Westwood with her famous *Pirate* collection of 1981 it gave British fashion a new lease of life. Self-producing fashion designers like Katharine Hamnett began operating from The Street, but very soon graduated to the

HABITAT, C 1967
A shop for switched-on people where the staff dressed in Quant and were coiffured by Sassoon

constituent of High Street activity. Moreover, they established the tradition of a spearhead minority. Based on their direct contact with the consumer they provided the incentive for renewal of the larger shops and department stores. In their wake came such phenomena as the shop within a shop beginning with the Way-In boutique at Harrod's. Also, boutique proprietors began selling their designs to department and chain stores, as in the case of Marion Foale and Sally Tuffin. From 1963 Mary Quant distributed her designs independently and on a large scale under the Ginger Group label.

High Street. In 1986 Hamnett opened in Brompton Cross a shop designed by the architect Norman Foster and watched her turnover of that year rocket to 4 million pounds.[12] Finally the transformation of Burton in 1979 signified a renewed interest in shop design.

The breakthrough proper came in 1982 when Conran and Davies salvaged Hepworth and recast it as the trendsetting chain store Next. The cool, chique interior with much exposed wood, glass, and chrome – and, very essential, a carefully positioned smattering of flowers – designed by David Davies Associates turned the shop design world upside down, and became the model for myriad other shops who applied it indiscriminately. On the heels of Next came Next Too, Next Essentials, and Next Accessories. Between 1983 and 1987 Davies launched women's and men's fashion, footware and accessories, home furnishings, cafés, florists', cosmetics, and lingerie – an entire lifestyle package for the aspiring urban consumer with flair. He began a mail order service too. How does George Davies account

PACKAGING WITH CORPORATE GRAPHICS FOR BIBA, 1963
John McConnell of Pentagram

for his success? 'Next was, is, and always will be about a team of people who get a lot of fun working together and are totally committed to design. And that means you're in love with the product you create.'[13] However, 'design' is not the only factor involved. Brian Johnson, director retail of DDA has pointed out that the attention to detail accorded Next shops, whether carrier bag or bouquet, underlines a respect both for the retail trade and for the consumer. Shopping he sees as a social, recreational activity. 'This sort of environment gives the client the urge to retain something of it on leaving. It arouses a basic human instinct.'[14] Shopping is a sensual affair of being seduced, of stimulated desires, of wanting and touching.

The Moroccan Joseph Ettedgui, originally a hairdresser, is a further major example of High Street 'design' fever. In 1984, at the time of opening a shoppers' paradise designed by Norman Foster in Sloane Street, he already had ten shops in Britain's capital. But it was the High-Tech atmosphere of the new building – cool sophistication, plenty of space, lots of chrome and rubber – that catapulted him into the front ranks of fashionable London. Nor, however, did he stop at clothes. Restaurants (Joe's Café) and mini-supermarkets (Joseph pour la Maison) were soon to follow. Their design – combining black and white, metal and glass – is the work of Eva Jiricna, who enhances their High-Tech look with an extremely refined and detailed finish. At Joseph's the central issue is, once again, lifestyle. 'Fashion is as much where you go, and how you organise your life', according to Ettedgui.[15] Here, fashion is what he is stressing, in doing so designating it the vehicle of the new style of shopping. But, for him, recreational spending comes into it too. 'My ideal kind of place would be a mixture of a café and shop, with regular clients.'[16]

From the atmosphere of these shops and the lifestyle concept it is but a stone's throw from fashion to the home, with accessories a step in-between. Besides Next and Joseph, Marks & Spencer indulged a change of course too. In 1988 it embarked cautiously on the sale of furniture, which for that matter is more neo and pseudo than modern. David Davies, whose office styled this department of Marks & Spencer, himself opened a shop offering fashion and furniture.

However, the waves of 'design' were destined to wash still further across the High Street.

Following in the footsteps of, and interacting with, the fashion chains came a whole series of designer boutiques such as those of Kenzo (by Jiričná), Hamnett (by Foster, and in Glasgow Nigel Coates), Issey Miyake (Alan Stanton and Paul Williams), Gaultier (Ron Arad, whose own shop should not be forgotten), Jasper Conran (Coates), and Yamamoto (Alfred Munkenbeck and Stephen Marshall). Shops selling 'design' accessories such as Ogetti, Fast Forward, Authentics, and Le Set supply the trendy consumer with all manner of indispensable gadgetry. Dining can also be done in style these days at 'designed' restaurants like Café Italien des Amis du Vin, Kensington Place, Bibendum, 51-51, Braganza, and the rest. In 1985 Harrods, Harvey Nichols, and other department stores set up 'design' orientated lifestyle shops concerned with quality, exclusiveness, and image. British Home Stores and Debenhams are revamping their interiors, with Harrods soon to follow suit. Marks & Spencer is recruiting many design consultancies like Pentagram and Conran Associates owing to its expansion into toiletries, wine, books, and records. The struggle to corner the yuppie market is in full swing, and there is no stopping 'design'. Recently subjected to it (and provided with interiors by DDA) were the Victoria and Albert Museum shop and the Design Council. And Fitch took under its wing Dillon's Bookshop, Esprit du Vin wineshops, British Telecom shops, and the Midland Bank.

The pampered consumer

Paradoxically enough the consumer – the reason all this upheaval began – is becoming increasingly difficult to pin down. Whereas at one time the choice of newspaper, use of leisure time, clothes, and car clearly spelt out one or other socio-economic group (and type of behaviour) today's consumer is no longer so easy to define. The trend towards individualism and a growing supply renders the target group increasingly smaller and more specific. Whereas 'youth',

BOOT AND SHOE COUNTER AT BIBA'S, 1973

to give an example, hitherto stood for a homogeneous group, it is now broken up into countless subgroups. In fashion, too, there has been no dominant style for a long time: anything goes, and in any combination. The consumer is able to choose from a multitude of styles (though he remains as restricted as ever to what is available). And yet the new shops seem to be aiming at the cosmopolitan, the well-informed, fashion-conscious buyer of about thirty. By 1990, according to the Henley Centre – which investigates future conditions for the retail trade – the number of young people between 25 and 34 will have risen by 7%.[17] At all events these shops are taking account of the recent phenomenon of young people with money to spend.

TOP SHOP IN 1970, 1972, 1979 AND 1982
the first three designed by Michael Howard,
Fitch-RS plc, the last done by Carlos Virgile of Fitch & Co.

In general incomes in Britain have risen, between 1976 and 1986 by no less than 25%. (And what of the consequences of Mrs. Thatcher's tax reductions for higher incomes announced in 1988?).[18] But more was bought on credit too, in 1986 to the tune of 30.7 billion.[19] Moreover the property boom meant an increase in buying products for the home. Rune Gustafson, responsible for marketing at Fitch's, estimates the total market at about 52 million people.[20] As this includes many older people, the struggle to claim the younger target groups is, he argues, particularly fierce. Another thing that strikes me, at any rate, is the great importance attached to having money, and to spending it. This may have something to do with the appalling unemployment situation in which work and money mean status. Whatever the case, it reflects British society as it is today, divided into the 'haves' and the 'have-nots'. On further reflection one could suppose that the fatal illness AIDS and a general lack of idealism and optimism – one only has to think of politics and its dwindling credibility – has fanned the hedonist flames. In the light of the many problems in the world today, people might prefer to retire to the seclusion of their own homes. Thorstein Veblen's analysis of almost a century ago of flamboyant mass consumption has truly come into its own.[21]

A report from 1987 on British lifestyles confirms, moreover, that 35% of adults see shopping as a pleasant way of spending their leisure time and have definite views about their shopping environment.[22] In any case, Britain's retail industries together with its design consultancies are well-prepared for the future. The predicted increase in leisure time will find expression not only in shopping as recreation, but also in, say, DDA's design commission for the DIY chain Do-It-All. The increase in the number of children under fourteen of a million in the coming ten years is already being met by large out-of-town children's department stores. DDA designed Kid Store for Woolworths, and Fitch Children's World for Boots. What intrigues me, however, is what design has in store for the 1.5 million additional 45- to 54-year-olds arriving within the next decade.[23]

So the prospects are more money and more leisure time; more shopping and more spending; and more status. 'Design', brands, and names act at all events as distinguishing factors. 'The new customer makes a great effort to look good. Image is high on their list of priorities. Where they buy is almost as important as what they buy', says press officer Nicky Cartwright of Harvey Nichols.[24] The latter condition has undoubtedly something to do with the social side of shopping – the question of where to be seen, and where to have lunch. Appearances are everything. Now that technical achievement and low prices no longer determine competition, quality and style are the twin focal points in marketing. And what is 'design' about if not these two elements?

The design arena

British designers have if nothing else been taking a good look at Japan where the shopkeepers take quality, style, and the wishes of the customer seriously. There individualism is such that shops have just one of everything 'on exhibit' – '*These* are just the shoes for you'! Sometimes even these are out of sight behind cupboard doors, so that the shop displays nothing but the interior design and – so expensive in Tokyo – the space. This shop-as-museum approach the British have taken over and modified.

In the shops of Hamnett, in Next and Joseph what matters more than anything else is style, atmosphere, and a jet-set 'feel'. The interior is far more important than the goods on sale, which fail to catch the eye with a daring eccentricity or through great originality. Although a complete upgrading leads on the whole to improved product design, we may go so far as to wonder whether quality in these cases remains in some sort of proportion to the price – Hamnett's cottonware, for example –. In this respect Davies' shop, in its attention to style and environment, represents a peak. 'Davies: furniture and clothing for a temperate isle' offers 'all those things which make English life so special.'[25] These include sturdy English knitwear and elegant furniture that evokes a feeling of the antique. Central to this shop is its *Brideshead Revisited* atmosphere, conjured up by such requisites as a rowing boat, old tennis rackets, cricket bats, spectacles and cigarette lighters from the thirties, much exposed

...aces in her day, Which she didn't want to waste away. She took the space
...built a castle in the air. On the turret she climbed up high, And cut a hol...
...e hole she built a boat, And put it in the castle moat. Sure enough came ...
...ugh the hole fell the moon. The moral of this story is, Nothing's out of re...

J O S E P H

LONDON SW1 **Joseph Pour la Maison** 16 Sloane Street **L'Express** 16 Sloane Street *Telephone 01 235 9869* **Joseph Tricot** 18 Sloane Street **Joseph Pour la Ville** 166 Sloane Street **Joseph Bis** 23 Brompton Arcade SW3 **Joseph Bis** 53 Kings Road **Joseph Bis** 124 Draycott Avenue **Joe's Cafe** 126 Draycott Avenue *Telephone 01 225 2217* **Joseph Bis** 130 Draycott Avenue **Joseph** 268 Brompton Road W1 **Joseph Pour la Ville** 13 South Molton Street **Joseph Bis** 14 South Molton Street **Joseph Tricot** 16 South Molton Street **PARIS Joseph Bis** 70 Rue Bonaparte 75006 PARIS **Joseph Tricot** 44 Rue Etienne Marcel 75001 PARIS **NEW YORK Joseph Tricot** 804 Madison Avenue New York NEW YORK 10021

ADVERTISEMENTS FOR JOSEPH AND HAMNETT
Style, atmosphere, and a jet-set 'feel' matter more than anything else

CHILDREN'S WORLD, 1987-88
Fitch & Co.,
A large out-of-town children's department store for Boots

QUANT'S MAKE-UP RANGE

most striking characteristic of designing in the eighties 'the process by which *everything* aspires to the condition of graphics: not just print or screens, but architecture, interiors and products.[30] The difference in terms of life expectancy is considerable. The outward appearance, a promise of its practical value; the gloss; the image – all these take the place of the product itself.[31] Nigel Coates describes modern life thus: 'The floppy disc has replaced the book; the telephone has barred the visitor; the credit card has done away with money; video has recorded the movie; tape music has become more real than live performance; advertising has sublimated the product.'[32] (Could this mean that competition will soon shift from between products to between advertisements?) Perhaps Mary Quant was right after all when she said: 'All a designer can do is to anticipate a mood before people realise that they are bored with what they have already got. It is simply a question of getting bored first.'[33]

timber, with a background of music and sounds of cricket. With this Davies is employing a form of anti-design, for those who want to be fashionable without being modern.

By giving priority to interior and atmosphere the British show themselves to be born salesmen and magnificent packaging designers. Prettying things up is their great strength. As a matter of fact DDA's first commissions were in packaging. I suspect that Britain's reputation as regards advertising plays a large part here too. The Public Relations value of 'design' and imagery is overpowering in the High Street. 'We export style', in the words of DDA's Brian Johnson.[26] Nor do other design consultancies mince words either. 'Without being too fantastic, a good designer can add style, fashion, entertainment, pleasure – call it what you will – but it is that little bit extra that makes one firm's products stand out and sell when set beside another's', according to Satherly Design Associates who describe the added value of design as 'that little bit of moonlight.'[27] The PA Design brochure states that 'the fundamental purpose of design is very simple: to differentiate a product or service from its competitors in order to improve profitability.'[28] 'Design' will sell anything – including, at times, next to nothing.

In his book on the sixties, Nigel Whitely concludes: 'All the applied arts – and in many cases the fine arts – aspired to the condition of fashion.'[29] The designer Robin Kinross names as the

INTERIOR ONE OFF, c 1982

DAVID DAVIES SHOP
*Offering all those things which make English life
so special in a Brideshead Revisited atmosphere*

chapter six   SOCIAL VALUES

The rapid growth of the big design consultancies and the overwhelming acceptance of 'design' as a means of improving sales seem to be at odds with the other side of design which historically speaking is inextricably linked with the profession, to wit, the social side. Great Britain was in fact the first country, in the person of William Morris, to link design with social responsibility. And what became of the legacy he left? The following chapters enter into the other underlying values associated in Britain with the idea of design. First to be discussed is the humanist side of design expressed in, say, the public sector. I will then tackle design ethics and the social ideals of British designers.

The state as client in the public sector

How has the government viewed its responsibility in the public sector from Ministry to airport? What has been its policy on design for the countless social facilities and services? Take the Post Office.
This major British institution has a long tradition of designer recruitment. In the thirties its first public relations officer, Sir Stephen Tallents, commissioned many famous poster artists like Graham Sutherland and Edward McKnight Kauffer, and film-makers such as John Grierson and Edgar Anstey produced outstanding documentary films. But these attempts were limited to direct public-relations material and individual commissions. And after the Second World War, too, there was little change in a policy that remained fragmentary and incidental. So the Council of Industrial Design was asked to advise, it is true, but merely on postage stamps. Only in 1968 could the Post Office's design policy be described as clear-cut and coordinated. In that year it enlisted the service of Stuart Rose as consultant designer on a fulltime basis, followed by Richard Stevens as design manager of Telecommunications (telecommunications having long formed a separate branch of the Post Office). Their function met with little understanding amongst their colleagues. 'Daily we had to redefine the reason for our existence', according to Stuart Rose.[1] And yet in 1976 the Post Office came up with a new and consistent corporate identity programme based on the alphabet designed by Banks & Miles. Its arrival, however, had less to do with any sudden comprehension of what designing was all about, than with the fact that in 1968 the Post Office had changed from a Crown-appointed Department to a private company.[2] This corporate identity seems to have little authority about it. Rose, for instance, had no say

UNDERGROUND STATION WITH A 1930s INTERIOR
Charles Holden, architect
A design policy unparalleled in its progressiveness

**SOUVENIR GIFT BOOK CONTAINING ALL THE
BRITISH POST OFFICE SPECIAL STAMPS, 1986**
Carroll, Dempsey & Thirkell
*Within the Post Office, the philatelic department is the only one with
an inspiring commission policy*

in matters of publicity, meaning that he was entirely dependent on goodwill in the application of the corporate identity here. Around 1985 the function of consultant designer ceased to be on an executive level and was relegated to the marketing department, commerce triumphing over intrinsic worth. Mike Dempsey, whose consultancy designs the special publications on stamps by the Post Office, has the impression that the philatelic department is the only one with an inspiring commission policy. He is unable to discern a general design-consciousness within the vast Post Office machinery.[3]

British Telecom has since become denationalised. Admittedly, it has made use of design in adopting a corporate identity. However, their advertising slogan 'It's you we answer to' contrasts painfully with complaints about call boxes that are out of order. The main outcome of denationalisation, which brought British Telecom's monopoly to an end, was more competition, with the commercial aspects uppermost to begin with.

For the London Underground, too, the Golden Age seems to be long past. Frank Pick, Vice-Chairman and Chief Executive of the

London Passenger Board in the thirties, managed to carry out a design policy unparalleled in its progressiveness. With the graphic designer Edward Johnston, who was responsible for the immortal sanserif typeface, the architect Charles Holden to design the stations, poster designers of the calibre of McKnight Kauffer and Charles Paine, and countless others, the multifaceted nature of this policy has yet to be equalled. Apart from material additions, such as by Misha Black's DRU in 1967, little has happened in the design field since those days. And so criticism of the doings and dealings of London's Underground continues unabated, while all London Transport can do is point to 'the lack of consistent policy towards urban public transport by the politicians, the lack of an integrated London Transport/British Rail strategy and the continued use and disguised subsidy of the private car.'[4] Its design policy became watered down, and was no longer centrally controlled. 'Everyone tended to do their own thing,' says Paul Moss, design manager of London Regional Transport.[5] Nevertheless this situation has since improved. Spurred on by the growing number of passengers, which shows an increase of 50% in the last few years, LRT reinstated in 1985 the function of design director. Moss points to public expectations and an increased awareness of marketing as the reasons behind this recent sympathy towards the role of design. The many accidents – the fire at Kings Cross in 1988 is an extreme case – will also have contributed to it. Thus it seems that design is being used here in the interests of the public.

Nationalised in 1948, British Rail (BR) got off to a good start by setting up the following year an architect's office to advise on architectural matters and designs. However, judging by the criticism levelled in 1955 by *Design* magazine, this would seem to have contributed little to an up-to-date policy or a coordinated design strategy. The need for these suggested itself only in the sixties, when DRU was able to effect the broadest of corporate identity programmes, extending from locomotive to uniform. A colour scheme, the logo of a double arrow, and the lettering designed by Jock Kinneir complete the picture. Over the years, however, both corporate identity and equipment have fallen victim to the ravages of

time. Dirty old diesel trains and delapidated stations are the result.

BR has of late woken up to the fact that its image is ripe for improvement. In 1980 it launched the prototype of the *Advanced Passenger Train* designed by Kenneth Grange (and with a tartan interior), and seven years later Jones Garrard and the Roundel Design Group were responsible for an entirely new identity for the Railfreight department. In doing so BR opted for a decentralised approach by division. Jane Priestman, formerly active with the British Airport Authorities as design coordinator, was approached to fulfil the same function with British Rail. BR has not remained aloof to the

POSTER FOR LONDON TRANSPORT, 1914
Tony Sarg

95

more commercial approach to design of the eighties, though the results are barely discernible as yet.

In direct contrast, London's airports have always had work in abundance for designers, as, with mounting pressure from an ever-increasing number of travellers, there is an ever-present need for expansion and adaptation. The British Airport Authorities (BAA), which manages Britain's airports, even received in 1969 a Presidential Award for Design Management. Until recently Jane Priestman worked at BAA as design manager at the head of a six-man strong team – although perhaps 'strong' is the wrong word, as there is so much work that most is passed on to design consultancies and firms outside the Authority.[6] The result is a lack of coherence and continuity, which has had both a positive and a negative effect on the terminals of Heathrow and Gatwick. On one hand they are spacious and open, on the other claustrophobically low and narrow; modern and efficient, but suffering from the living room effect of the

CORPORATE IDENTITY FOR RAILFREIGHT, 1987
Michael Jenny, John Bateson, Harold Batten and
Chris Bradley of Roundel Design Group
a decentralised approach by division

obligatory – and thus typically British? – incongruously coloured carpeting. Here, too, the question arises of whether designers working in association with the BAA will be capable of ensuring that the airports age gracefully, rather than prematurely. In any case, Dick Peterson, unlike his predecessor Jane Priestman, is on the board of directors. For him it is not so much a matter of enforcing a BAA identity. 'It is more a question of managing a standard of design, making sure that the overall quality is high and that BAA get good value for money.'[7]

Of the Ministries little has been heard in the field of design since the sixties. This was when the Ministry of Public Building and Works was commissioning designers on all sides, one result being Jock Kinneir's signposting of 1967 for Britain's roads. Although their printed matter is well taken care of by the design department of Her Majesty's Stationery Office (HMSO), a distinguishing corporate identity and a more service-orientated approach are still conspicuous by their virtual or complete absence.

Although this overview does not pretend to be complete, it gives some idea of the British State in the capacity of client; its policy has often been casual and half-hearted. Within government bodies design has yet to be institutionalised. Why has this vitally important area been so neglected? In the first place, the designers working inside these departments are but a tiny cog in a vast, unwieldy, complex machine that makes coordination and decision-making even more difficult than usual. Henrion stated in 1965, that no less than fifteen authorities within the Post Office were involved in the design of a telephone call box![8] Effective management in the traditional structure of the civil service is as good as impossible. Thus the consultancy PA International concluded in 1980, with London Transport in mind, that there was 'a lack of skills required to run a large business.'[9] Often designers are not operating on the level where the decisions are made and consequently have little say in them. As Stuart Rose puts it: 'Just give us a few guidelines on design, old boy, and my people will carry it out.'[10] In other words, designers are not often taken seriously.

Then there is the strong feeling of hierarchy of the civil servant

CORPORATE IDENTITY PROGRAMME FOR BRITISH RAIL, 1965
Design Research Unit
One of the most comprehensive corporate identities in Britain,
extending from locomotive to uniform

who has no intention of taking risks and upsetting his superiors – an attitude come across at other levels of Britain's class society. Rules and political tension leave little room to move. Thus James Holland claims in an article on the State as client that the success of the Ministry of Information, specially set up for the Second World War, was due to the very fact of its non-permanent character. This meant that it could bypass rules, or at least bend them a little. He is also of the opinion that the proliferation of committees with their characteristic mentality is responsible for the lack of individual enterprise. 'In the matter of design, committees tend to be scared by the unorthodox and prefer to play safe. They would rather deal with organisations than with individuals, with groups, units, partnerships or other multi-headed set-ups. This ensures anonymity to both sides

CORPORATE IDENTITY FOR BAA, 1986
John Lloyd and Jim Northover of Lloyd Northover

LOCO 89, 1983
Kenneth Grange of Pentagram, Brush Electrical Machines Ltd.
steel chassis with aluminium and GRP cladding
To date one example has been made as commissioned by British Rail
and is currently being tested in service

to a design contract; nobody need eventually be personally responsible for anything – the organisation man's ideal.'[11] British indirectness, a strong sense of politics and hierarchy, and a fear of things new would appear to stand in the way of any integration of authorities and designer.[12] Is Great Britain 'a sullen, lumpen, dirty, cold and deceitful nation which hates serving anyone except its betters, especially the rich and the titled', as critic Peter Dormer argues?[13] Any social motivation in promoting the use of design, certainly in the case of the government, has yet to make itself apparent.

There are, however, signs that design will infiltrate further into the administrative world. Government institutions, denationalised in ever-increasing numbers, will have to start 'thinking commercial', and present themselves as both with-it and businesslike. Corporate identity is a relatively easy way of coming across as a friendly and efficient enterprise. A new image, with an up-to-date look, can have a great psychological effect on staff and public alike. The Department of Trade and Industry and that of Transport and Employment, plus organisations like the Metropolitan Police, Social Security, and political parties are already ahead in this respect. The 'High Street design' effect is undoubtedly making its mark on government circles in Britain. This could well mean that the designer's task will be whittled down to simply producing an image. We may only hope that the commercial pressure of denationalisation leads to a more extensive service, and to more consideration for the general public.

The Morris ethics take effect

What happened to the social values first exhibited by British

98

designers in the nineteenth century? And what did they consist of?

A moralistic element made its debut in the applied arts with John Ruskin, who evaluated everything in terms of the society engendering it. 'The book I called The Seven Lamps was to show that certain right states of temper and moral feeling were the magic powers by which all good architecture, without exception, has been produced.'[14] He denounced the alienation of man, who was condemned to degrading and soul-destroying work behind the machine. 'And the great cry that rises from all our manufacturing cities, louder than their furnace blast, is in all very deed for this, – that we manufacture everything there except men; we blanch cotton, and strengthen steel, and refine sugar, and shape pottery: but to brighten, to strengthen, to refine, or to form a single living spirit, never enters into our estimate of advantages.'[15] These ideas hark back to the analysis of capitalism by Karl Marx, who described this process of alienation as follows: 'Within the capitalist system all methods of raising the social productiveness of labour are brought about at the cost of the individual labourer; all means for the development of production transform themselves into means of domination over, and exploitation of, the producers; they mutilate the labourer into a fragment of a man, degrade him to the level of an appendage of the machine, destroy every remnant of charm in his work, and turn it into a hated toil; they estrange from him the intellectual potentialities of the labour-process in the same proportion as science is incorporated in it as an independent power; they distort the conditions under which he works, subject him during the labour-process to a despotism the more hateful for its meanness; they transform his lifetime into working-time, and drag his wife and child beneath the wheels of the Juggernaut of capital. But all the methods for the production of surplus-value are at the same time methods of accumulation . . . of capital. Accumulation of wealth at one pole is, therefore, at the same time accumulation of misery, agony of toil, slavery, ignorance, brutality, mental degradation, at the opposite.'[16]

We of this age, indoctrinated by a written history of design that places the machine on a pedestal, are apt to forget just what enormous, far-reaching, and also negative consequences capitalism

had for those times. Moreover, mechanisation introduced wage labour to the applied arts too. The division of labour resulting from mechanisation demoted the artist-designer to a pattern-drawer. The artistic object for use was turning into an article of mass consumption. No longer was its design determined by style, whether national, contemporary, or personal, but by the law of supply and demand. Mechanised production implied that supply would indeed come before demand, with all its consequences, commercial and otherwise.

This picture of a society ruled by production and profit Ruskin countered with that of creative work, of the craftsman. He found that

IT WAS F.H.K. HENRION WHO FIRST PUT THE UNION JACK ON BEA'S (BRITISH EUROPEAN AIRWAYS) LOGO IN 1969

architecture and applied art had to exhibit their individual nature –
in other words, that they were made by people. Without that
personal touch the result, he concluded, was worthless. This aspect is
brought out in his book *The Stones of Venice* (1851), which became the
bible of the Arts and Crafts movement.[17] But Ruskin put his ideas into
practice too, initially as teacher at the philanthropic Workingmen's
College, and later at the St. George's Guild, which he founded in
1871. Many artist-craftsmen with ideals would follow him in this.

To this moralistic and humanistic reaction William Morris
added a sequel in the applied arts. He considered the well-being of
decorative art to be in direct proportion to the healthy and happy
experience it gave the artist to make it. 'Real art is the expression by
man of his pleasure in labour.'[18] He rejected the distinction evolved
through the ages between work and pleasure, work and art. Art *for*
the people had also to be art *by* the people. Paternalism, such as was
later to return in the Modern Movement, was foreign to his nature.
His ideal was the cooperative Medieval community – as he saw it, a
community in the true sense of the word, and not governed, as in his
day, by competition.

Being less a theoretician than a man of action, Morris put his
ideas to practical effect. Against the machine-made products of
inferior quality he set his own hand-made objects for use. He did so
initially with friends through the firm they founded together in 1861;
later it would come under his charge as Morris & Co. Beginning with
stained-glass, furniture, and embroidery he later added books (the
Kelmscott Press), textiles, and wallpapers (the Merton Abbey
workshops). The tragic fate of these superior, and therefore
expensive, products is that they ended up with the very social
stratum whose lifestyle and mentality Morris so vigorously opposed,
the well-to-do middle class or bourgeoisie. However, for Morris, and
for others of the Arts and Crafts, the priority did not lie with the
consumer. His ideal was not to turn out well-designed mass-produced
goods, nor to reject the exclusive product, but to achieve as high a
quality as possible.[19]

Over the years it became increasingly apparent to Morris that
neither an atelier nor poetry could change art and the world, so he

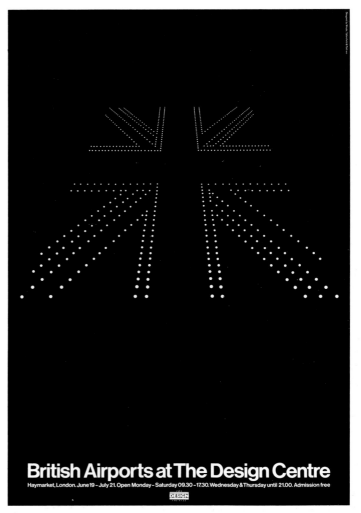

EXHIBITION POSTER FOR THE DESIGN COUNCIL, 1978
Brian Tattersfield of Minale, Tattersfield and Partners

acted accordingly. He embraced Socialism, then a new movement, contributing to it work of great consequence. He saw little credibility in taking the road of gradual, parliamentary change. 'Individual men cannot shuffle off the business of life onto the shoulders of an abstraction called the State.'[20] Only a revolution could alter society for the better. And ultimately, doing worthwhile, creative work implies an influence of the working man over the means of production. Morris also realised that a revolution cannot take place on a social and economic level alone, but demands a moral revolt too. E.P. Thompson sees that as his greatest contribution, 'the appeal to the moral consciousness as a vital agency of change.'[21] For the applied arts it was his humanism, his attention to the welfare of the individual, that was important. Other British artists were to take up Morris' ideas.

C.R. Ashbee was another who considered satisfying work seminal to craftwork and put this into practice at his School and Guild (later Guild only) of Handicraft. For example, he engaged his craftsmen not on the strength of their capabilities as such, but rather from their personality. In 1902 Ashbee, along with his wife and twenty-seven workmen and their families, moved to the little village of Chipping Campden, in search of the ideal lifestyle. 'Essentially', concluded Alan Crawford in his extensive study of Ashbee, 'the Guild was an attempt to enrich the lives of working men through the values of art in the broadest sense.'[22] Most members of the Arts and Crafts movement, however, were not that politically aware (although many flirted with both Socialism and Fabianism). What they did, rather, was to adopt individual expression as an essential condition, and pursue further Morris' design principles. Printers and typographers, too, were to extend a pleasure in work, and in a first-rate product, well into our own century.

The last-named group in particular was well represented within the DIA – perhaps it was they who brought along Morris' precepts. Thus the DIA pamphlet *A modern creed of work* of 1916 was still speaking in Morris' language. 'It [good design] never is good unless both designer and workman do their best for the sake of doing it. . . The delight in doing a job well for its own sake is just as natural to

IDENTITY FOR THE DEPARTMENT OF EMPLOYMENT, 1988
John Lloyd of Lloyd Northover

man as greed or laziness or fraudulence. . . But the excellence of an industry depends, first of all, on the religion of the workers, on their religion or workmanship. It will excel if they do not produce merely to sell, if their first aim is to make the best article possible . . . when the aim is merely to sell, the workman, the designer, even the middleman, is bored with his work. He thinks of nothing but the struggle for life; and life itself has no significance for him. No man is

NEW UNIFORMS FOR LONDON UNDERGROUND PERSONNEL

living well unless he feels the significance of life in his work and not merely in his pleasures; and the community which is not living well will be overcome by the community which is, overcome in material things no less than in spiritual.[23]

Between the two wars the social ideals became watered down. What remained was the emphasis on simplicity, honesty, and good workmanship. This part of the legacy – more an approach to design than a social ideal – was to remain long in evidence; combined with the pleasure of making things in craft production, and with the slogan 'fitness for purpose' in industrial design. During the thirties the two groups parted company through which the bond between craftwork and industrial design was severed. A succession of government organisations, the first founded in 1920, focused on the industrial designer, and craftwork moved into isolation. Only in the work of Herbert Read did something of a moral concern about

quality, honesty, and sincerity in art and life continue to sound at the time, as in his book *Art and Industry* of 1934.

New disputes?

It was only in the fifties that new ideas and discussions about the role of the designer broke out once more, motivated by the ideas of the so-called Independent Group. This was an association of artists, architects, and theoreticians who between 1952 and 1955 came together at the ICA (Institute of Contemporary Arts). They were rebelling against the artistic climate of those days, and the conservative reactions to the Americanising of Britain which was bringing the consumer society that much closer. The members of the Independent Group, amongst whom Richard Hamilton, Reyner Banham, Peter Blake, and Lawrence Alloway, were, in their admiration for both American popular culture and technology, the founders of Pop Art. Hamilton was the first artist to treat elements of popular culture as fine art.

Their view of the design world – then still happily ensconced in 'fitness for purpose' and the 'right' choice of materials, and directed by production methods – broke all the rules in the book. Banham propagated a throwaway aesthetics and 'planned obsolescence' to counter the idea that product design should strive towards a universal, permanent value. 'We are still making do with Plato because in aesthetics, as in most other things, we still have no formulated intellectual attitudes for living in a throwaway economy. We eagerly consume noisy ephemeridae, here with a bang today, gone without a whimper tomorrow – movies, beachwear, pulp magazines, this morning's headlines and tomorrow's TV programmes – yet we insist on aesthetic and moral standards hitched to permanency, durability, and perennity.[24] He argued in favour of a greater sense of reality, on realising that designers should acknowledge social change. They had to climb down from their pedestals and see to the needs of the consumer. The example he always gave was the American automobile, the last word in styling and planned obsolescence, and all those other – at least in the eyes of design purists – acts of barbarism. 'Don't forget that the automobile is more than just a means of transport – it is a badge of rank, and the common man's toe-hold on the marvels of technology – and the iconography or its ornament must be able to say all of those things.'[25]

In other words, there was to be a greater connection with the product's emotional and symbolic aspects. Hamilton endorsed this view, but went further in his ominous predictions, such as the image of the designer as a 'specialist in the look of things', and 'designing the consumer to the product.'[26] The last-named he compared, to a storm of protest in the colums of *Design* magazine, with fascism, salesmanship, and education: a sharp retort indeed. Had not the CoID continually tried to turn consumers through education into design consumers?

Protests against the depreciation of the profession, the reduction of designer to prettifier, and the creation of still newer packaging for products could be heard in Britain too. In 1963 the graphic designer Ken Garland called for 'a reversal of priorities in favour of more useful and lasting forms of communications' and hoped that 'the prior call on our skills will be for worthwhile purposes.'[27] Yet this did nothing to solve the real problem, that of the two faces of design. For dependence on the client and on the commercial outcome leaves no room for a critical, compromise-free attitude. And in serving a system of overproduction, waste, fooling the public, or whatever else one cares to call it, that one 'well-designed' flatiron is not going to make much difference.

Attempts to tackle other burning issues of the sixties and early seventies such as pollution, energy consumption, waste of materials, and the like were few and far between. When *Design* magazine launched a series of articles in 1967 on 'environmental design' it concentrated on the technological, analytical interpretation. More psychologists, sociologists, climatologists, and other researchers was its motto. Victor Papanek, the American who advocated 'design for the real world', was paid attention enough. In 1975 'fitness for purpose' for a time became 'fitness for need'. In the words of Misha Black: '"Fitness for purpose" is as appropriate a slogan today as it was half a century ago, but we must now evaluate the purpose before deciding whether it justifies the search for a solution which will fit it: an elegant bomb is still a bomb.'[28] These utterances seemed to make little impression. In general they were not followed up.[29]

What did happen was that both designers and CoID re-evaluated their opinion of the profession. As Paul Reilly, director of the CoID, was forced to admit: 'We are shifting perhaps from attachment to permanent universal values to acceptance that design

JUST WHAT IS IT THAT MAKES TODAYS
HOMES SO DIFFERENT, SO APPEALING? 1956
Richard Hamilton, collage, collection Kunsthalle Tübingen
The instigator of the British Pop Art movement

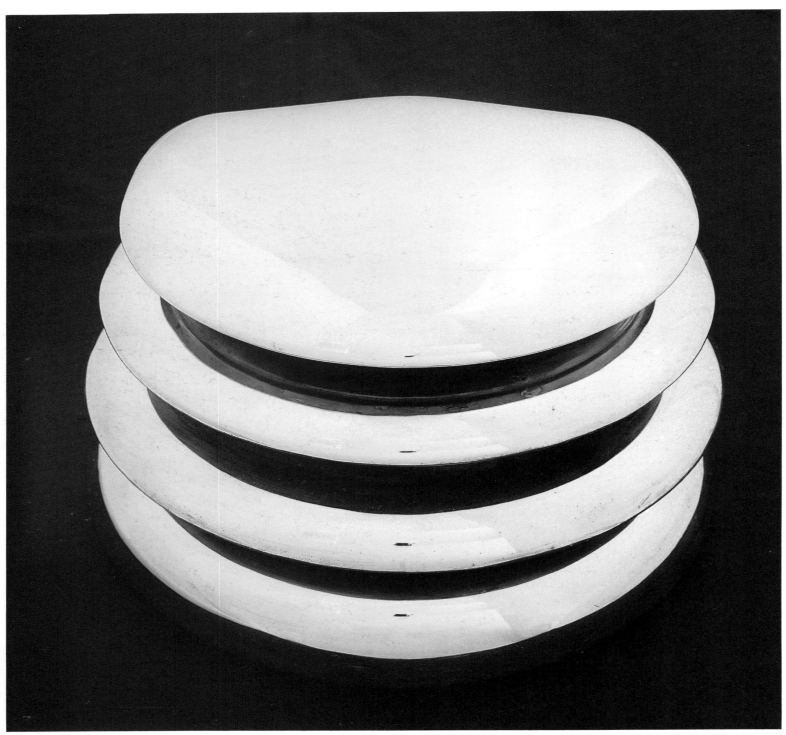

CONVECTOR FIRE, 1934
Christian Barman, His Master's Voice, chromium-plated steel,
collection Sheridan Coakley SCP, London
Fitness for purpose questioned

ON TO JAPAN, 1945
Sevek

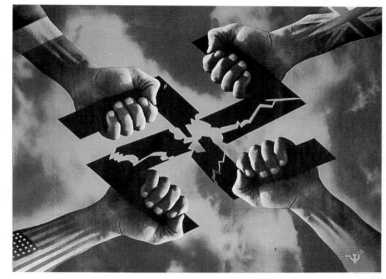

POSTER, 1943
F.H.K. Henrion

may be valid at a given time for a given purpose to a given group of people in a given set of circumstances, but that outside those limits it may not be valid at all.'[30] Christopher Cornford acknowledged an 'insufficient awareness of the symbolic (or discursive, or semantic) role of *all* human artefacts.'[31]

And yet these sporadic, idealistic sounds soon died away, as they did elsewhere, to the advantage of efforts towards the acceptance and professionalisation of design. Italy is the only country where discerning architects and designers have been able, or have been enabled, to keep coming up with new design theories. Most others have gone no further than the fact that their work is there to be sold. To resort to Banham's realism: 'Whether the styling offers those hilarious old chromium speed-whiskers, or the soberest and staidest Good Design, the message is always: 'Buy me!'.'[32]

In recent years critics like Peter Dormer, Peter Fuller and John Thackara have indeed come forward with new scenarios as regards the role of design in twentieth century society. They reject the rational designer governed by machines and money. '. . .too much of today's design is informed by the belief that capital and machines are more important than people, a division of labour between thinking and doing that is reinforced by professional self-interest – the 'keeping the experts expert' syndrome.'[33] On the strength of the effects of modernism they reject the ethics of production. Dormer and Thackara argue in favour of a critical stance towards technology, and for a return to the soft, sensual qualities in industrial design. For them, craftwork is not only an advance guard for mass production, but can in itself be a worthwhile contribution to industrial production. The strong points of British craftsmanship,

such as knowledge of materials, a feeling for quality, and creativity, they would like to see assimilated in industry. Peter Fuller is approaching Morris' ethics from a new angle. Instead of an unquestioning subjection to modernity, machines, technology, and progress with the appropriate need to control and rationalise, he advocates an 'ethic of "livelihood", which celebrates the unity in diversity of nature, and our place in it.'[34] We seem to have come full circle.

LIVERPOOL BENCH, 1984
Ron Carter, Miles Carter, English ash
The ethic of livelihood for the public sector

'The practical commonsense of modern society . . . is the natural genius of the British mind. . . The bias of the nation is a passion for utility', said the American essayist and poet Ralph Waldo Emerson when visiting Britain in 1847.[1] Besides social values, British design is greatly influenced by usefulness, matter-of-factness, simplicity, and a relative lack of outspoken ideologies. This is apparent in the first place from the British approach to design and the definitions of 'good design' briefly discussed in Chapter One. That British designers have both feet planted fairly and squarely on the ground is further evidenced by their reactions, mostly unfavourable, to more extreme foreign trends. The latter do not fit into the image they have of designing. Moreover this reserved attitude towards influences from abroad strengthens their insular position. In this chapter I will be looking at the more sober sides to British design in relation to the more extreme influences.

In his *True Principles of Architecture* of 1851 August W.N. Pugin advanced the two principles that from that time on were to have a dominant influence on British design: '1st, that there should be no features about a building which are not necessary for convenience, construction, or 'propriety'; 2nd, that all ornament should consist of enrichment of the essential construction of a building.'[2] In other words, 'ornament your construction, but do not construct your ornament.'[3] Pugin influenced Henry Cole, who with his Summerly's Art Manufactures wanted to rid the everyday object of all inappropriate elements. He set out to achieve 'superior utility which is not sacrificed to ornament.'[4] So water jugs were painted with waterlilies, and a bread-knife given a handle in the shape of an ear of corn. Cole and his circle interpreted the appropriateness of ornament very literally indeed. They took to an extreme usefulness and fitness; straightforwardness and expression of function; and, not only for Summerly's Art Manufactures but for all Arts and Crafts practitioners, craftsmanship.

This practical aspect, this 'doing-as-designing', is expressed most fully by Morris, who by studying historical methods and from his own experiments became proficient in such wildly diverse areas as glass painting, embroidery, wood-carving, pottery, bookbinding, weaving, and carpet-making. 'A designer', he stated, 'should always thoroughly understand the process of the special manufacture he is dealing with or the result will be a mere *tour de force*. On the other hand, it is the pleasure of understanding the capabilities of the special material, and using them for suggesting (not imitating) natural beauty and incident, that gives the *raison d'être* for decorative art.'[5] Ashbee

INGRAM CHAIR, 1900
Charles Rennie Mackintosh
Splendid isolation

also considered the practical aspects priority number one, followed by humanistic, expressive, and aesthetic qualities. The crux of the matter remained the adding of decoration to a fundamental function or construction.

At the turn of the century Crane and Lethaby disseminated further the Arts and Crafts principles as teachers at the Royal College of Art. They laid special emphasis on the individual, and on expression and experiment, in other words a craft-based education: the school as studio. To this Lethaby added as essential a thorough knowledge of tools, materials, and processes, in doing so setting the precedent of design as a problem-solving activity. 'Art is not a special sauce applied to ordinary cooking; it is the cooking itself if it is good.'[6] No wonder, then, that the design approach taught there exercised a powerful influence on members of the DIA and other designers that would continue into the thirties.

BREADKNIFE, 1848
Felix Summerly's Art Manufactures
Joseph Rodgers & Sons, ivory, metal,
collection Boymans-van Beuningen Museum, Rotterdam

PLATE WASTE NOT WANT NOT, 1840-50
A.W.N. Pugin, Minton, earthenware,
collection Boymans-van Beuningen Museum, Rotterdam
Ornament your construction, but do not construct your ornament

But many years after that as well, craftsmanship and designing based on 'making' were to remain a widespread approach. In the definitions of 'good design', too, which in the long run were to replace the theory-based principles of designing, the practical aspects are unmistakably present. The historian Patrick Nuttgens stated at the 1986 International Design Conference at Aspen that designing in Britain had been characterised until well into the fifties as follows: 'Good design was concerned with everyday ordinary things; it was unpretentious, sometimes rustic in character, would reveal good craftsmanship, was vernacular (that is, local, regional or national, rather than international) and the product of common sense rather than unique genius.'[7] With this it would seem that during the course of a century little has changed. 'The character 'Englishness' in design', as Peter Dormer observed in 1985, 'consists partly in a lack of overt ideology or polemic; but it is also the result of evolutionary rather than radical development.'[8] Sobriety and realism are part and parcel of design in Britain. What can we learn from the reactions of the British to foreign trends that brought them face to face with more radical ideas?

Outside influences

In the nineteenth century the *Art Journal* used to complain that the British would rather copy a Continental design than think one up themselves; on the other hand it expressed its pride about home achievements, as borne out by the following: 'The French themselves are struck, as well they may, with the useful and popular direction taken by the industry and ingenuity of England, as compared with those of France, so exclusively devoted to the enjoyments and tastes of the very rich.'[9] The designing of luxurious, extravagant products evidently appealed little to the British. This is just as apparent from their reactions to Art Nouveau. The Arts and Crafts practitioners, for all their influence on the non-British Art Nouveau movement, were bitterly opposed to it. Crane spoke of 'a strange decorative disease', and Ashbee of 'German squirm' and 'Glasgow spook'.[10]
After exhibiting work by Mackintosh and his Glaswegian circle the Arts and Crafts Exhibition Society decided that once was enough. Evidently they found these artists too extreme. C.A. Voysey described Art Nouveau as 'out of harmony with our national character and climate.'[11] An incorrigible chauvinist, he never left Britain's shores, and repeatedly expressed his abhorrence of extraneous styles. 'Each country has been given its own characteristics by its Creator and should work out its own salvation. The best architecture in the past has always been native to its own country.'[12] For him a house was a home, and would never become 'a machine to live in'.

The wealth of ideas propagated by Pugin and Ruskin, who in fact proclaimed the Gothic – a style that originated in France – as the true national style, were still very much active amongst Arts and Crafts practitioners. For them the ideal of personal and highly individual expression was sacrosanct. Individualism hindered British

WATERJUG, 1847
Richard Redgrave for Felix Summerly's Art Manufactures
J.F. Christy & Co., enamelled and gilt glass,
collection Boymans-van Beuningen Museum, Rotterdam
Waterjugs were painted with waterlilies; Cole and his circle
interpreted the appropriateness of ornament very literally

111

DISPOSABLE PAPER CHAIR, 1964
Peter Murdoch, International Paper, laminated paperboard
The influence exerted by the 'swinging sixties' has made little
impression on product design, except for the odd item of furniture

designers from adopting other influences, while the design principles of straightforwardness and an appropriate handling of ornament held them back from undue extravagance. In 1900 the display by the Victoria and Albert Museum of donated Art Nouveau furniture caused such a storm of protest that it was decided to remove it. Since then the museum has not acquired one single piece more in this style. The writer and prominent DIA member Noel Carrington was having trouble with Art Nouveau as late as 1976: 'Personally, I must own that I still find its [Art Nouveau's] lush, curvilinear exuberance very sickly, and the decoration of Mackintosh's much-praised Glasgow tea-rooms, with their elongated females and chairs, very near to a nightmare.'[13]

Then there is the Modern Movement, with which the British were quite unable to cope. 'We do not understand this modern movement in design and we do not like it,' said the weaver and textile designer Minnie McLeish in her review of the Leipzig Fair of 1927.[14] For Lethaby, Cubism and the Deutsche Werkbund were an offence to the eye: 'Personally I hate it, but it was not done for me.'[15] The critic John Cloag spoke of the 'Robot Modernist School' which he condemned as 'utterly inhuman' and 'fit for machines, not for men.'[16] 'Foreign', 'outrageous', 'cosmopolitan' and 'Bolshevik' were other derogatory terms given the Modern Movement.[17] Satirical jokes about the tubular steel chair were the order of the day. And for the authors of *How to Live in a Flat* 'the ultra-modern living room' seemed to be 'a cross between an operating theatre, a dipsomaniac's nightmare, and a new kind of knitting.'[18]

Arts and Crafts and the machine

The lack, or very late arrival, of a Modern Movement in Britain is often associated with the question of acceptance of the machine. Thus Gillian Naylor states that British designers discovered far too late that their ideals could be realised with the aid of mechanised production. Moreover, this discovery came, according to her, 'more or less as a personal revelation, there was no attempt to formulate a

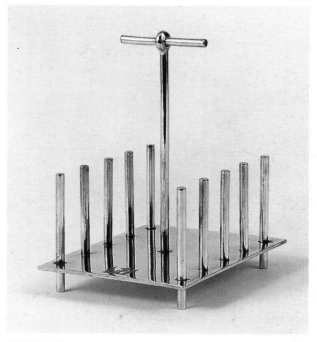

TOAST RACK, 1878
Christopher Dresser, Hukin & Heath, silverplated, collection Boymans-van Beuningen Museum, Rotterdam

corporate theory until the establishment of the Design and Industries Association in 1914.'[19] But the fact was that British Arts and Crafts practitioners did not adhere to the view of their continental colleagues, based on a mass-produced, high-quality, classless product. What mattered much more to them was one that was well-made and honest, and whether it was made by hand or by machine was irrelevant. Several of them, including Pugin, Voysey, and Crane, did in fact make designs for factories.

While most designers did accept the possibilities offered by

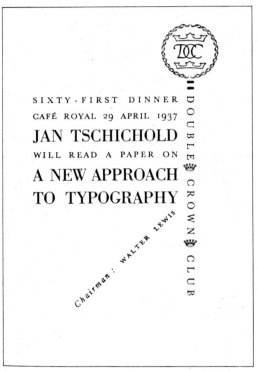

MENUCARD OF THE DOUBLE CROWN CLUB
on the occasion of Jan Tschichold's visit in 1937
It demonstrates how little Tschichold's ideas and those of the Modern Movement
generally were understood in England at that time

machinery, their attitude towards it remained essentially the same. Ashbee, for example, said as late as 1918: 'Machinery untamed . . . that is the barbarism we now have to fight . . . the accursed conditions of industrial machinery in which we live . . . the tyranny of mechanism . . . we know that the great mechanical interests, the large factory organisations . . . are against us . . . the slavery of the

machine . . . the corrosive influence of mechanical power.'[20] It was still largely because of the social consequences that the Arts and Crafts practitioners refused to accept the machine at the beginning of this century. The question remains as to whether this point of view can be termed negative. For not accepting, or in truth half accepting, the machine most writers of design history tend to label this movement anachronistic and conservative. But to me it seems much more to attest to a critical disposition that did not lapse into mere slavish adoration as was the case in, say, Germany. British artist-craftsmen treated industry with a healthy dose of scepticism. Rooted in a British respect for tradition and continuity, but also because influential Arts and Crafts practitioners like Lethaby and Crane continued to dominate the educational side, these ideas were destined to die hard.

It is probable that the individualism of the artist-craftsmen proved a barrier to embracing industrial production. Crane, principal at the Royal College of Art, argued in favour of spontaneity, instinct, and subjectiveness instead of systems, regulations, and objectiveness. And as the rational approach was the very essence of mechanical production, it had more immediate need of the latter properties than of the former.

Compromise

Modelled on the Deutsche Werkbund, the DIA included amongst its members artist-craftsmen as well as manufacturers, retailers, architects, and industrial designers. Its ideas reflect considerable uncertainty as regards the Modern Movement, which in its yearbooks is at times vilified and at others praised. Thus in 1918 the editors of the DIA magazine could write: 'The last thing we should father is this idea of standardisation, which would surely kill all local individuality and expression,' only to state a few paragraphs later that its most pressing duty was 'to satisfy the requirements of the great majority.'[21]

This ambiguity, partly the result of the great diversity amongst it members, deprived the DIA of the strength to get the 'efficiency

CHAIR, 1933-34
*Gerald Summers, The Makers of Simple Furniture, laminated birch
except for Scandinavian design, which did appeal to British designers,
most foreign streams got the cold shoulder*

DE LA WARR PAVILION, 1935
Erich Mendelsohn, Serge Chermayeff
A continental, International Style building designed by two Marxist
Jews for a socialist Earl in an ultra right-wing town for retired
colonels and civil servants

style' off the ground. The 'pots and pans brigade', as it was known, had a small, hard core of idealists who of their own free will strove for a better day-to-day environment. Its non-political disposition, the lack of means, and the disunity amongst its members held the energies of the DIA in check. The image gained from the book by Noël Carrington, who as an active member experienced the DIA from close up, is that of a convivial, amateurisch club whose aims remained obscure. Only the sober slogan 'fitness for purpose' was common to all its members, and was to long reverberate in British ideas about design.

DIA members were down-to-earth in other respects too.

M.H. Baillie Scott and Alfred Simon, for example, harboured no illusions as regards being able to educate the public. 'Those who live in villas expensively furnished as well as those humbler folk, whose conception of the ideal house centres in a bay window adorned with lace curtains, and fenced from the road, say with a cast iron railing picked out in blue and gold . . . As long as people can get cheap and flashy smart-looking things to put in their houses they will choose such things.'[22]

The German emigrant and staunch champion of the Modern Movement, Nikolaus Pevsner, in evaluating the work of DIA members wrote that 'the positive was still neo-Georgian rather than modern', and missed an uncompromising, modern, rational style.[23] The point of view of the theoretician Herbert Read is equally inconsistent. While throwing doubt on the notion that a functional, efficient product is by definition beautiful as well, he also maintains that 'Our machine design, our engine design, our transport design, our electrical design, are among the best in the world and slowly the influence of these dominant industries will filter down to pots and

DINING TABLE AND CHAIRS, 1936
Marcel Breuer, Isokon, bent plywood
The Modern Movement in Britain

116

pans, to furniture and fabrics.'[24] Here he is once again using functional design as jumping-off point and guiding principle.

Unlike in other countries the Modern Movement in Britain was not borne by architecture. In the 1920s British architecture was dominated by so-called 'Neo' styles. According to Charlotte and Tim Benton the official exhibitions on architecture by the Royal Academy showed compromise, while modern architects steered clear of social housing due to the lack of status associated with working for the government. They too suffered from lack of unification and had no clear-cut opinion on the Modern Movement. Only a handful of private individuals gave them a chance to build and then only because they saw the Modern Movement as a novel, exotic style.[25]

The stylistic aspect of the moderns seems to have dominated British discussion more than its actual content. 'We want neither a new or universal style, we should know nothing about styles', says Seddon.[26] Uniformity was evidently taboo amongst the British individualists. Newman states that modernism was accepted only when it became fashionable in the thirties, and then in the Art Deco variety.[27] The flood of emigrants (Pevsner, Gropius, Breuer, Moholy-Nagy, Mendelsohn, Chermayeff, Lubetkin, Gabo) were a further help in ushering in acceptance of the Modern Movement at that time. But by then it was past its prime, and when Breuer and Gropius left for America in 1937 the British Modern Movement gave up the ghost.

In conclusion we could say that mass production and the Modern Movement were too extreme, and too abstract, for the British – and perhaps too much of an overstatement. Its visual logic, its well-reasoned nature, was a far cry from everything Britain's designers had been brought up on. There, design, from Morris onwards, was more a matter of actual doing and making than an intellectual exercise. Their rejection of dogma will have played a role here too. Nor, I suspect, did the socialist leanings of Modern Movement philosophy appeal to them.

Pop and Memphis

After the second World War influences from America in particular

SATIRE ON TUBULAR STEEL FURNITURE
by the authors of the book 'How to live in a Flat', 1936

were difficult to ignore, especially the principles of 'styling' and 'streamlining' (or 'Borax', as it was termed in Britain). Then there was the general agreement, promoted by the Council of Industrial Design, on what 'good design' was. Gordon Russell describes it in the debut issue of *Design* magazine in 1949 as follows: 'Good design is not a luxury . . . Good design always takes into account the technique of production, the material to be used, and the purposes for which the object is wanted. Good design is not precious, arty or high falutin. Good design is not something that can be added to a product at a late stage in its planning or manufacture. It is fundamental.'[28] Faced with this functional, sound approach such extremes as Borax and styling stood little chance, as evidenced by a market research report from 1961 into British product: 'The people abroad still regard us as a country dominated by our past. Our goods are seen as reliable but old fashioned, utilitiarian and expensive.

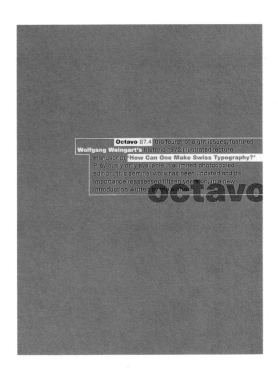

OCTAVO MAGAZINE
8vo

They have a reputation for durability and are even regarded as being "virtually indestructible". But they are felt to be "constructed with too much of an eye to efficiency in use and too little to their appearance".'[29]

Nevertheless Britain produced in Pop its own extreme movement which, based in fashion and street culture, launched its assault on the design world, where it was given a mixed welcome. '. . . The movement has been far too derivative, picking up various styles and techniques from art nouveau and Odeon 20s through to pseudo space age, regenerating them without moving on from them

with any sense of creative purpose; it often uses decoration so inappropriately that, however brilliant the original concept, it detracts from its own raison d'etre.'[30] The absence of originality was a particularly damning aspect. On the other hand, *Design* appreciated its non-moralising, non-dogmatic approach. Pop was a shot in the arm for British designers, for 'design' was now in the public eye, yet at the same time it went against universal ideas on what design should be. The resulting backlash was an argument in favour of a return to basic, rational design as advocated by Misha Black, with greater emphasis on the scientific approach. The influence exerted by the swinging sixties has made little impression on product design, except for the odd item of furniture.

The same goes for the revolutionary ideas of Alchimia and Memphis who at the end of the seventies caused a sensation with their agressive, radical designs. There was enough fuss, both for and against, but little influence. However, in the eighties, individualistic designer-makers challenged the sobriety of British design in their own way.

Island or sponge?

British designers have always been quite unequivocal in their reactions to foreign streams. Except for Scandinavian design, which did appeal to them, they all get the cold shoulder. What is striking here is that it is chiefly the stylistic aspects which trigger this off. Matters of content hardly come into it. 'Just act normally – that's quite unusual enough' would seem to be the general consensus of opinion. The ideal of the good industrial product for everyone did reach Britain, but has made no real headway amongst designers of its class-conscious society. It seems to place them in a dilemma. They have, admittedly, taken it up from the Northern countries but only halfheartedly, as if it were incompatible with their own ideas. 'Utility' and 'sound workmanship' are as far as it goes.

Design as the British see it reflects in its doing-as-designing mentality and its individualism more of a practical foundation than an intellectual one. Only now – at a time when designing can be for wholly commercial ends, and the direction taken by the theoretical side of the profession as a whole is anything but clear – British designers, working through the giant design consultancies, are gaining enormously in strength. Perhaps it is the very lack of an articulated intellectual background that has left the way open for them.

In largely dismissing foreign trends, however, the British are faced with the question of their own identity. What are they proposing in their place? Considering the ever-recurring criticism, sparked off by exhibitions and presentations of British design, or by

market research into the reputation of the British product abroad, this is a problem. And the government has been hammering away for a century and a half for more 'design' for the benefit of export. But in doing so they only increase the confusion between 'doing what everybody else does' and working towards a British identity. *Blueprint*

VODKA BOTTLE LABEL FOR ASDA WINES & SPIRITS, 1987
Mary Lewis of Lewis Moberly Design Consultants and Dan Fern (illustrator)
Synthesis of influences

magazine confirms this problem when it states that 'Good industrial design, when recognised by the public, is international in origin . . . as a cause, industrial design is best served by internationalism – not by proclaiming the joys of Britishness. Industrial design cannot save Britain, but only internationalism can save industrial design.'[31]

British practice would seem to prove *Blueprint* right. Adaptation to trends and design in other countries and in general has been more than substantiated during the eighties by the giant design consultancies. Their designs look as if they could have been made anywhere. This very balance between insularity and absorption is again a specifically British phenomenon: the capacity to assimilate is on one hand a positive strength, yet it can also mean the absence of a British identity.

The other great exception to the rule of insularity is British graphic design, which attests to a veritable flood of foreign influences. Emigrants from America (McKnight Kauffer, Robert Brownjohn, Bob Gill, Tom Wolsey) and those from German speaking countries (Hans Schleger, Ernest Hoch, F.H.K. Henrion) helped professionalise it and breathed new life into it. Swiss, German, and Dutch typography set graphic design well on the road towards becoming a rational,

organised, systematic profession. Americans have strengthened the humorous side in graphics and advertising. It is here that the British,

NOMOS OFFICE FURNITURE, 1986
Norman Foster of Foster Associates, Tecno Italy, chromium steel, glass, collection Boymans-van Beuningen Museum, Rotterdam

thanks to this very influence from abroad, seem to have arrived at an individual style that mediates between the extremes, and whose synthesis is its most persuasive attribute. In the chapters that follow I shall be treating this development more exhaustively in the shape of such typically British phenomena as the designer-maker and designing for the media.

BOOK COVERS FOR FABER & FABER, 1985
Carroll, Dempsey & Thirkell

TOKYO CHAIR, 1985
Rodney Kinsman, OMK Design Ltd., steel, collection OMK Design Ltd., London Japanese, Italian, French, or . . . British?

In the last decade the British media have been referring to an unprecedented revival of the crafts.[1] The attention has not focused so much on the amateur craftsmen or those working in the tradition of familiar forms, but rather on the artist-craftsmen. New galleries and existing art institutions have been showing brash objects made by iconoclastic youngsters who mock all limits to their particular fields. The potter has become a ceramist and artist in clay; the designer a designer-maker of haute couture objects which just happen to allow being sat on. Where did this development come from and how should we view it? What does the blurring of the boundaries between design, craft and art mean?

Gender confusion

The new trend has caused quite a rumpus. This is not only because of what seemed to be a sudden explosion of creativity, but chiefly because it threw doubt on current notions regarding the fields of design, craft, and art, and brought with it considerable uncertainty as to their identity. Just as in British pop music these upstarts with their androgynous objects were responsible for a form of gender confusion.

No-one seemed to know anymore where they stood. In attempting to introduce some clarity and to define the area covered by this chapter, it is essential that we take a look at some terms and concepts. Interpretation of words like *design, crafts,* and *art* is, after all, not fixed for all time, but is evolving – the meaning of these terms has grown historically. Historically speaking, the distinction between autonomous, fine art and the applied arts arose with the arrival of the manufacturing process where products were partly or wholly made by machines. This process called into existence the division of labour, with which for the first time designing and making could no longer be done by one person. The terms and concepts which appeared at the end of the eighteenth century reflect the differences between the fine and the applied arts, as shown by Wolfgang Pilz.[2] *Arts and crafts* stresses the manual and material as opposed to the fine arts as a mental creation. *Applied art* emphasises the functional as opposed to the liberal and autonomous, and the production of goods against the creation of ideal values. *Industrial art* stresses the mechanical aspect, as distinct from the inspirational creative process of the artistic genius in making a unique work of art. Thus applied art is material, functional, and produced manually and/or by machine. All these concepts reflect, moreover, the underestimation suffered by applied art in comparison

UNIE CHAIR, 1986
Floris van den Broecke, Annelies de Leede, Furniture Makers,
plywood, steel, upholstery, collection of the designer
Designed for Café De Unie in Rotterdam, it was unfortunately
rejected in favour of Starck chairs

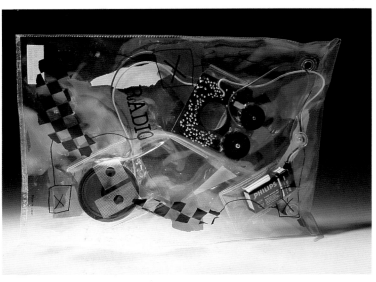

BAG RADIO, 1981
Daniel Weil, Apex Inc., Japan, PVC,
collection Boymans-van Beuningen Museum, Rotterdam

with the fine arts.

Looked at so far we could say that products assessing a practical value and partly or wholly machine-made belong to applied art. In this process the designer is the one who thinks them up, but does not make them. This has led through the years to what Norman Potter calls the 'white-collar' designer who works for a company, full-time or otherwise, and devises for it new products and models.[3] Thus designing is a conceptual activity with no dirty work involved. The conceptual and intellectual as distinct from the manual; division of labour against design and construction in one process; working for an organisation instead of independently – these, then, are the differences between designer and craftsman. So far, so good. However, this convenient arrangement is thrown into confusion and doubt, when assessment and values are introduced, and in particular with regard to borderline cases. When does an object of utility become applied art?

The answer, according to eighteenth century art theory as formulated by Kant, is when this occupation is not labour but rather recreation, or leisure time activity. The craftsman who exercises his trade in order to live, whether smith or potter, is, in these terms, not practising applied art. Here art theory contradicts itself, by considering mechanically produced implements as applied art on one hand, and rejecting them as such, because wage labour is involved, on the other. This contradiction, as I see it, can be traced back to the difference between inventing and making. The inventor of a thing is considered on a higher plane than its maker (mental as distinct from manual work). This brings with it, besides that of fine versus applied arts, a further distinction, that between concept and execution.[4]

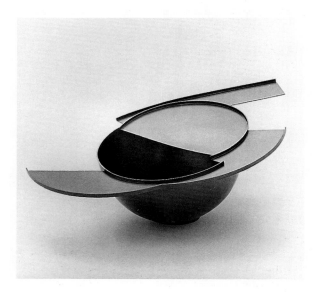

BOWL, 1981
Michael Rowe, red brass, patinated dark brown

VASE, 1985
Carol McNicoll, earthenware
collection Boymans-van Beuningen Museum, Rotterdam
Probing the limits of the pot shape

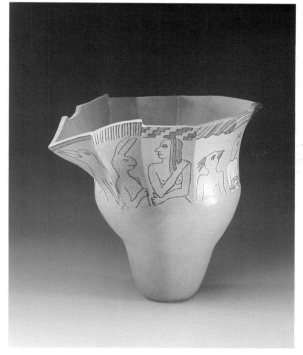

VASE, 1978
Alison Britton, earthenware
collection Boymans-van Beuningen Museum, Rotterdam

The criteria that subsequently appeared in applied art were every bit as much a product of their age, and got in the way of establishing clear-cut definitions. For art that was not autonomous the practical value or functionality was the all-important criterion in the eighteenth and nineteenth centuries. Following on from these historically evolved interpretations we can then say that every product that refers to a function or specific purpose does not belong to the fine arts but to applied art, and of these products all that are not conceptual come under craftwork. That the idea of 'usefulness' has been the decisive element in evaluating applied art is chiefly due to Gottfried Semper. He summarised the products of this field (by then divorced from the fine arts) as the result of purpose, material, and technique, thus stressing the material aspects. Far into our own century the applied arts would be appraised according to these standards, which were quite different from those in the fine arts – not in the final analysis thanks to Functionalism.

The universal claims of the Functionalists have, however, made way for heterogeneity and decentralisation – no longer the masses and an international validity, but the individual and a specific nature. Rationality has had to go under in favour of irrationality.
The concept 'function' has in the last few decades broadened from just meaning operational to include the symbolic, the emotional, the individual. Because of this the distinction between applied and fine arts has come under heavy fire.

The borderline cases – partly autonomous, partly functional –

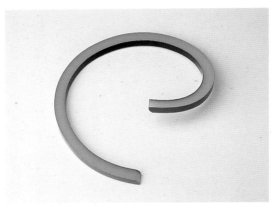

NECKLACE, 1980
Susanna Heron, acrylate
collection Stedelijk Museum, Amsterdam

CONTAINER, 1987
Julia Manheim, papier maché
collection Stedelijk Museum, Amsterdam

add their own confusion to that of the identity of applied art. From the sixties onwards jewellers and potters have been stepping out of line by exploring the limits of usefulness in their field. Jewels have become extensions of the body, and impossible to wear: teapots can no longer pour and just stand there looking out of the ordinary. Yet in all these cases function remains the point of departure and central theme, also when the maker is obsessed with its denial or with the broadening of its meaning (e.g. by stressing the personal expression element). This is why I feel that these objects still belong to the applied and not the fine arts.[5] An attendant difficulty is that all these fields – ceramics, glass, jewellery, textiles – have developed in very much their own way. Each demands considerable foreknowledge for one to be able to judge the objects they produce. Incidentally, this does confirm once again the absence of binding theories or ideologies in the applied arts as a whole.

The confusion is not entirely dispelled, however, for what, we may ask, is the difference between arts and crafts and design?

126

WINGNUT CHAIR, 1984
Jasper Morrison, cardboard
Put together on its existing machines by a factory that normally
fabricates laundry baskets

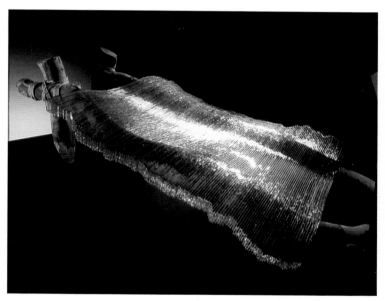

ANGARAIB CHAIR, 1987
Danny Lane, clear float glass

The method of production (one-off against serial, handmade as distinct from machine-made) would at first sight appear to be the answer. But this does not say enough, particularly when we realise how many hybrid forms are involved. The dinstinction made earlier between concept and execution seems to clarify the matter much more. Thus work which is all execution with no single conceptual springboard attached, for example because it carries on an existing tradition, I would classify under craft as a trade. Purely conceptual work involving no execution I would then call industrial design. And everything in-between is arts and crafts. The two first-named categories do not concern us in this chapter. The third is seminal to it and includes, another cause of the confusion, as many practitioners from the craft world as those trained as designers. In Britain the first are called 'artist-craftsmen' and the second 'designer-makers'.

MUSIC STAND, 1986
Fred Baier, aluminium, steel, sycamore
private collection

From woolly socks to trendy yuppies

Victor Margrie, until recently director of the Crafts Council, states that the difference between artist-craftsmen and designer-makers is that the latter cannot boast a philosophical basis.[6] In doing so he is saying that the designer-maker is a recent phenomenon that did not necessarily originate from the crafts. The craft world, which in Britain testifies to a remarkable and strongly identified continuity, has indeed arrived by other routes at concepts comparable to those of the designer-makers. Potters in particular adopted a stance detached from the developments in designing and from this isolated position attained their own values and norms.

In the thirties the craft potter Bernard Leach brought studio pottery to a new level, stressing simplicity, tradition, and workmanship. He was inspired by the 'eternal values' of Oriental ceramics. At that time the crafts were very much associated with the countryside and good living, and were promoted as such: honest, individual, reliable, British, and rooted in tradition. After the Second World War the promise of a better life gave the crafts a fresh boost. Magazines on the crafts agitated against over-industrialisation, while the war had reinforced the desire for individuality in the fifties. Anti-materialism, the appeal of simplicity and nature, and conservatism remained major characteristics of the craft world. 'If the crafts are about anything', according to potter Hans Coper, 'they are about the way we, as individuals with different skills, abilities and desires, can shape the way we live.'[7] The energy crisis of the seventies, concern for the environment, and rejection of the consumer society and the large-scale lent strength to the 'small is beautiful' mentality. The crafts were engaged, according to Christopher Frayling, in making objects in natural materials (preferably beige-coloured) which were functional, made by one person from a traditional design, rural, non-fashionable, easy to understand, long-lasting, and consoling.[8]

But by then a countercurrent, that sought a rapprochement with the fine arts, was already underway. Even in the years preceding the Second World War the potter William Staite Murray was claiming the status of work of art for the pot, scattering further the

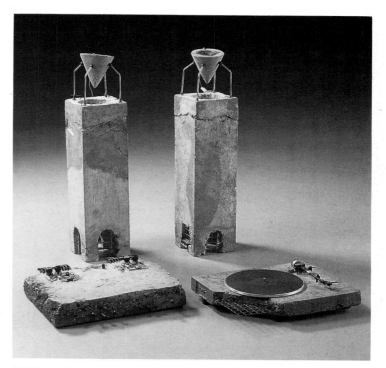

CONCRETE STEREO, 1985
Ron Arad, One Off, London
collection Boymans-van Beuningen Museum, Rotterdam
A reaction against black-box design

seeds of the coming confusion as teacher at the Royal College of Art. Peter Fuller places the beginning of the reaction against the conservative craft tradition at the end of the fifties. Influenced by Lucie Rie, Hans Coper, and the American West Coast ceramics, the new generation expressed increasing concern for 'the liberation of the clay', the word 'ceramics' came to be used instead of pottery, and violating the rules became the principal driving force, as exemplified

BANGLE, 1979
Caroline Broadhead, nylon tufts in silver-covered wooden hoop, collection Sara Rilkard
Plastics, feathers, and fabrics have made their entrance

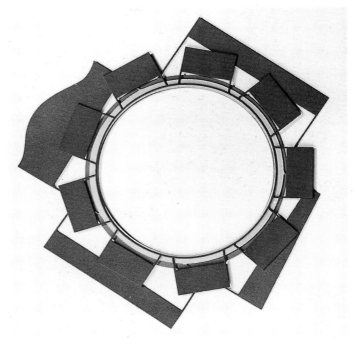

VOYAGER, 1984-85
David Watkins, wire, wood, neoprene, collection Stedelijk Museum, Amsterdam
Objects that carry their relationship with the human body to extremes

by Alison Britton and Carol McNicoll.[9] No longer did they cling to the traditional notion of function. Britton speaks of a group 'concerned with the outer limits of function; where function, or the idea of a possible function, is crucial.'[10]

In the seventies the alienating elements became increasingly dominant. The exhibition The Craftsman's Art held in 1973 in the Victoria and Albert Museum presented the crafts primarily as objects. No longer did they console, while improving society as an ideal was old-hat. Crafts was a challenge, a language with which to express

oneself as artist – the pot as domestic sculpture. The revelation that 'even a modest domestic utensil can also be a target for some emotional or intellectual expression; a micro-culture of potential meaning', as John Houston put it, was beginning to dawn.[11] In the words of the textile artist – or should I say, textile maker – Annie Sherburne: 'When I work, I feel that I am finding a map around myself. I want to know things I didn't know were there, and find expression for explosions of feeling. I try not to let my right hand know what my left is doing, until a line, colour or form suggests

SWAN, 1987
Matthew Hilton, SCP Ltd., aluminium

itself, then a conversation can begin.'[12] Could this mean that the arts and crafts functions as personal consolation for its maker?

From now on, the craft ideal would be the vehicle for personal expression, a means of embodying an idea. The influence of conceptual art, which rates the idea higher than its realisation, has had something to do with this; according to some because it heightened the desire for concrete, tangible things. The frame of reference for crafts practitioners became much wider. The generations raised on the art schools that proliferated in the sixties are busy exhausting the inspirational possibilities of the fine arts. And yet their overriding concern remains their own field, albeit in the form of probing its limits, as Britton does. Here, as in other areas of British design, tradition is still the pivot around which everything else revolves.

This is visibly the case not only in ceramics but also in the world of jewelery, which began gathering momentum at the end of the sixties. Influenced by Dutch and German developments and performance art, the British ornament is no longer the precious item – ring, earring, bracelet, brooch, necklace – in gold or silver. Plastics, feathers, and fabrics have made their entrance, and are worked into objects that carry their relationship with the human body to extremes. Jewellers like David Watkins, Julia Manheim, Susanna Heron, and Caroline Broadhead are making short work of the taboos dogging their profession. Textiles were to follow suit, taking the form of decorative, expressive, personal objects.

Reinforcing the craft tendency towards the fine arts was the arrival of government bodies such as the Crafts Council in 1971 (known then as the Crafts Advisory Committee), and the new galleries. In that same year Ralph Turner and Barbara Cartlidge opened the Electrum Gallery 'to promote modern jewellery as an art form.'[13] Two other galleries, Detail and Aspects, followed in its wake. The craft world was trading in the rural scene, woolly socks and all, for that of the city-based, trendy yuppies, and was gaining self-confidence into the bargain.

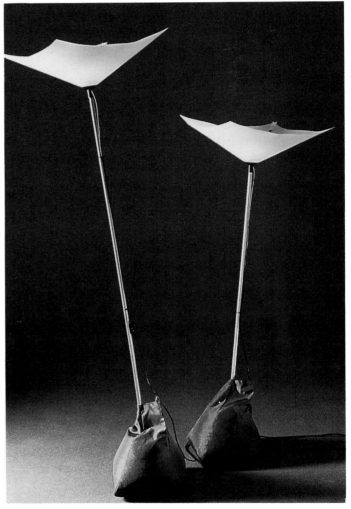

TALLO LIGHTS, 1971
Jane and Charles Dillon,
B.D. Ediciones de Diseño, Spain

Designer-makers

Students trained as industrial designers also began demanding more freedom during the sixties, as evidenced by, amongst other things, the general criticism levelled at the RCA, which was accused of turning out more artist-designers than engineer-designers.[14] In those days the borders between art and design were vague, and the Principal, Robin Darwin, noticed a preoccupation among the students with the 'rediscovery of themselves as individuals.'[15]

On top of this search for more individuality they questioned the validity of working for industry. 'The reaction among young designers against the idea of a career in industry has been widespread, and many students have turned their backs on acquiring the skills which are necessary for industrial production' observed *Design* magazine in 1975.[16] Students like Robert Welch, David Mellor and John Makepeace – not necessarily from the RCA – opted for social or idealistic reasons for making their products themselves. But there were more reasons for doing so, for example remaining self-employed and staying in contact with the shop floor.

According to Tony Stokes who in 1987 organised an exhibition on art and craft that featured a new generation, these were also people 'who don't want to be told what to do, and who don't want to work to commission.'[17] As Ron Arad puts it: 'I didn't want to follow up my training at the Architectural Association by first spending ten years at an architects' office.'[18] In 1980 he opened his own shop, One Off, selling his own work and that of like-minded colleagues. Jasper Morrison declined the idea of a 'marketing ploy of huge dimensions, calculated to sell a product by covering it with a skin which smells of design. No one finds this smell as bad as the designer, whose good intentions are sliced in two and sprayed matt black.'[19] So some of the individualistic designer-makers have also been reacting in their own way to what in Britain has in the late eighties become the very big business of design.

However, this does not always mean they are anti-industry. Very often this opting for studio production is born of necessity, owing to a lack of response by industry. Thus Floris van den Broecke, one of the first designer-makers, says: 'At the time when I trained, I would perhaps have liked to end up working as a staff designer for a large scale furniture manufacturer. But the problem, then as now, is that there are so few firms that actually employ furniture designers. One has to make things oneself, if one is going to see them produced at all.'[20] The same goes for Ralph Ball, Jasper Morrison, Matthew Hilton, and others. Ironically enough the designer-makers are almost single-handedly responsible for innovations in the field of furniture in Britain today. Sometimes this leads to economically viable studio production; sometimes to commissions from foreign manufacturers, as in the case of Jane Dillon, who saw her designs realised on an industrial scale in Italy and Spain.

Not only does studio production guarantee attaining the quality one wants, but also allows for the possibility of developing new materials and techniques (up to a point, of course) as Jan Kaplickly and David Nixon set out to do when they founded Future Systems. The results of their investigations can be seen in their furniture. In the work of Fred Baier, too, the desire to push the use of wood to its limits is everywhere evident. Other designer-makers, like André Dubreuil and Tom Dixon, have ended up in this role by chance. In 1984 the sculptor Tom Dixon learned to weld so he could repair his motorcycles. Later he did this on stage with scrap metal as a form of entertainment in the Titanic Club begun by him. This led to an exhibition and commissions. Nigel Coates became involved as an architect in the interior design of a Japanese restaurant, and, as a logical next step, designed and made its furniture.

Craft for craft's sake?

One of the most striking motives of the 'makers' – to give them another, more neutral name – is their desire for personal expression and meaning. In spite of all its consumer affluence and technological progress, modern society did not necessarily bring us any increase in happiness or health. Ideals and expectations have evaporated into

HORSE CHAIR
*Nigel Coates, Rockstone, Japan, metal
designed for the Japanese Metropole restaurant*

134

thin air. The disillusion and the feeling of emptiness have generated a longing for new symbols. As the ceramist Angus Suttie put it: 'I hate the way things are going at the moment. My work is saying, 'I don't agree, I don't believe in what is happening'. It is a reaction *against*. The government is stripping everything down to function. But life is richer than that. So I am looking at ritual things and in my work putting on things that have no relation to function.'[21] Incidentally, it is not for nothing that so many 'makers' seek inspiration in exotic cultures and historical styles.[22] A comparable *cri de coeur* for more emotional footing came from groups like Alchimia and Memphis, which was responded to on an international level. But when there is no longer a common symbolic order, can you then provide one with pots and chairs? The need for meaning can, out of necessity, only be satisfied on a small scale, in the most personal of domains. This relates also to the reaction of retreating to an area that is limited, conveniently ordered (by oneself) and free of problems.[23]

In their longing for personal expression the makers are voicing a definite individuality, and are claiming more freedom than their predecessors had. They are doing so formally by breaking down borders and removing taboos, but in another sense too, in their desire for emancipation into the fine arts. It also seems to be a status question. Breaking formal constraints has become a separate quality of the applied art work. And because of this individuality, servitude, in the sense of complying with a tradition or fulfilling expectations, is put to the test.

For designers, the turbulent Italians were offering some sorely needed variation to the dull, dreary, rationalised products with which industry was swamping us. The servitude of working for a client or patron has been brought into dispute. As opposed to their intrepid predecessors who professionalised and established design, today's designer-makers have no wish to be unquestioning yes-men. What they want in place of a programme of requirements is more imagination and expression. Industry, which after all the economic problems is more and more averse to taking risks, appears an increasingly unsuitable place for creative and self-willed talents. So in all this, there is evidence too of a reaction to foregoing generations.

TROGGLE ROPE CHAIR, 1987
Julienne Dolphin-Wilding, stressed pine, nautical rigging
Weathered furniture from recycled materials, keeping technology down to the minimum

135

CHAIR, 1988
Tom Dixon, Dixon P.I.D., steel and rush

choosing, is that the makers will get stuck with it. Stigmatised and shunned on all sides, their path will be the dead-end street; while their talents deserve better that that. Without access to new techniques and possibilities the designer-makers will not get much further. Fortunately, there are now signs that the designer-makers are about to infiltrate industries – albeit mostly foreign ones. The artist-craftsmen run the risk of remaining trapped in the 'ghetto' of a select public that buys expensive decoration, or admires it in a gallery. When maintaining craft skills and the attraction of the handmade product are the only reasons for the continued existence of these objects, they are doomed to the realm of relics and nostalgia.

Now, of all times, the level of liberation plus all the attention should, to my mind, lead to more freedom and a true breaking down of the boundaries between the industrial and non-industrial spheres. Furthermore, these phenomena and developments seem to me to indicate a reappraisal from within the profession itself, or rather from its branches, in the quest for new beginnings. I feel that both processes could have an effect that would only be positive and valuable.

This reaction, however, is not confined to Britain only. It is a general one occurring in other countries as well. The British reactions seem to be much more individually motivated, continuing the tradition of dissent, rather than being part of a movement, stream, or specific generation.

The danger of such an attitude (the results of which are well-covered and lavishly illustrated in the ever-proliferating number of glossy magazines) whether or not this position is of their own

BED
Daniel Grey, wood, collection Tim Burke, London
Anti-design design

chapter nine   **DESIGN FROM THE STREET**

Alongside the traditional values bound up with British design history and craftsmanship, design in Britain has received a powerful stimulus from less historically burdened sources, such as the street and youth. This 'street style' or 'youth culture' – it could do with a better name – which has been evolving since the fifties, has had a tremendous influence on fashion, music, magazines, advertising, television, and video. It has been attacking the established order of things in bursts, bringing innovation with it. During the last ten to fifteen years this has been evident in the British fashion revival, the countless new trends in designing record sleeves and magazines, and the recent field of pop videos. It is a visual culture, geared to style, most perceptible in the media, and having a strongly commercial character. In this chapter I shall attempt to map out the influence of British 'youth culture' and discover the Britishness in the related media.

Youth culture, club culture

Youth culture is to be found everywhere; that is, in Western countries which have reached a certain level of prosperity, through which young people have become a target group for commerce and industry. Key words in this respect are Coca-Cola, jeans, T-shirts, and music. What makes British youth culture so special and what is its influence on design?

The youth of Britain is distinguished from that of other countries by its obsession with style. For Britain's young people style is a way of communicating, but it has become an end in itself as well. Its twin motivating forces and principal issues are fashion and music. British youth culture is very much a result of the country's class structure, for it is before anything else a working class culture, a street culture. We only have to think of the countless pop musicians, from the Beatles to the Sex Pistols, who made their way from the city slums to the hit parade. Thus the author and observer of youth culture, Peter York, relates British youth's obsession with style to the deprivation it suffers. 'Deprivation throws you in on yourself, on clothes, hair, music and dancing, local clubs and developing taste in a few things to an obsessive degree.'[1] For this social group, from the seventies onwards shunned by society to an increasing degree, style is a matter of vital importance in which every detail counts.

While in the fifties this lack of influence on day-to-day life was compensated for by spending money and having fun, in the seventies

**NEVER MIND THE BOLLOCKS
HERE'S THE SEX PISTOLS, 1977**
Jamie Reid, Virgin Records
Blasphemous treatment of Queen and Country

GOD SAVE THE QUEEN RECORD SLEEVE, SEX PISTOLS, 1977
Jamie Reid, Virgin Records

it took a much more serious form. The postwar social optimism was on the wane, and unemployment and the deterioration of Britain's economy at that time served to strengthen the feeling of disillusion and frustration. Punk, the movement that caused such an upheaval in its day, began according to Peter York as 'liberal bashing, hippie bashing'.[2] And yet the anarchy of punk was largely non-political and symbolic. It was a stylistic form of protest; although the symbolism in its blasphemous treatment of Queen and Country was political, and

the British tabloids did their level best to inflate punk into a national threat. York points out that, besides getting less education and fewer opportunities, Britain's youth is more coherent and less materially-minded that that of, say, America.[3]

However, the visual anarchy of punk did not come from the street alone. A second major source was the fine arts, as a reaction by the new generation to its predecessor. Jon Savage, who has worked for the magazine *The Face* since its inception, says: 'Early punk wasn't proletarian or even protesting, It was an art movement, reminiscent of nothing so much as an English version of The Factory, Andy Warhol's 60s forcing house.'[4] Malcolm McLaren, who together with the self-taught designer Vivienne Westwood opened in London the first punk shop, Sedationaries, was an ex-art student. The musicians David Bowie and Brian Ferry were educated at Newcastle University where they studied under the artist Richard Hamilton.[5] Around 1974 McLaren and Westwood, who had managed to focus all attention on Sedationaries by continually changing both the shop's name and its contents, hit on the idea of starting a pop group as a vehicle for their ideas and designs. This group was to become the notorious Sex Pistols. In general British art school students have much feeling for developments in the music scene. That means that in Britain the street (pop music and fashion) and the fine arts (the art schools) are inextricably linked. Many graphic designers, such as Malcolm Garrett and Alex McDowell, started off by working for unknown pop groups on their record sleeves, videos, and the like. And conversely, celebrated pop musicians like David Bowie, Adam Ant, and Boy George had the outfits they wore on stage during their theatrical performances made by young fashion designers. Music, which has been the expressive outlet of Britain's youth all along, brought the street and the art school together.

The term 'street style', which repudiates the art school side and places the accent on style, is to my mind only partially successful as a description. The word 'youth culture', on the other hand, has closer connections with the commercialising of initially small-scale, creative activities. It is here that working and middle classes clash. Former Sex Pistol Johnny Rotten (John Lydon) blames this rift for the group's demise. 'Working class implies you must be unintelligent, but working class people do have a sensibility and McLaren doesn't understand that', he explained recently in a programme televised by the BBC.[6] 'We were manipulated by the record business companies and particularly by the press . . . That's all we are: it's just product going down.'[7] So there is indeed a considerable difference between the street culture and High Street culture. If 'street style' and 'youth culture' are linked to different things, then these terms are inadequate

DRESS AND JACKET, WINTER 1983
Vivienne Westwood, pattern designed by Keith Haring, wool, bracelet by Tim Binns
collection Het Nederlands Kostuummuseum, The Hague

in expressing today's stylistic innovations. As I see it, it was the coincidence of punk street anarchy with the art school's creative energy that brought about innovation in British design in the fields of fashion, textiles, record sleeves, pop videos, magazines, and advertising, as an ever-widening stream.

Fashion

At the beginning of the eighties fashionable London was simply brimming over with excitement and energy. Suddenly British fashion designers were back in the picture on the international circuit.

In 1984 the clothing industry was a major British money-spinner and employer with an export value of 1.2 billion pounds.[8] Thatcher's reception at 10 Downing Street during Britain's Fashion Week served to underline this economic importance and brought recognition to the profession. Journalists and buyers came to the capital in droves; foreign magazines wrote of the New London Look; and young fashion designers became celebrities overnight. What did the innovations in British fashion consist of, and where did they come from?

Humour, youthfulness, unexpected twists – sometimes making the article impossible to wear – individuality, and eccentricity are the hallmarks of fashion as designed by Vivienne Westwood, John Galliano, John Richmond, and Maria Cornejo. According to *Blueprint* the strength of British fashion lies more in eloquence than in elegance. 'British clothes speak of rebellion, ideology, and group

AUTUMN/WINTER COLLECTION 1988-89
John Galliano
Flaps and points are everywhere

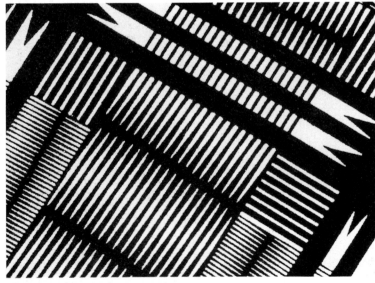

COSMIC CHECK TEXTILE FOR BODYMAP LTD., 1984
Hilde Smith

identity. The French and the Italians on the other hand have the hang of the fabric and know how to enhance and tease the body with it.'[9] Westwood herself describes it thus: 'Street fashion has become a known quality, a classic style with its own motifs: flaps and points are everywhere, so are clothes that don't follow the lines of the body and are even diametrically opposed to its curves and bulges.'[10] This British style, many-layered, draped, and above all theatrical, with all its decorative and non-traditional elements, created a

HAND AND PILLAR, 1986
Timney-Fowler, Timney-Fowler Ltd., cotton

SMALL ROMAN HEADS, 1986
Timney-Fowler, Timney-Fowler Ltd., cotton

talent, as the result of the high level of training and the amount of give and take at the art schools between the fine arts, textiles, and fashion.[13] Thus the group calling itself The Cloth consisted of four textile designers trained as painters, while Grahame Fowler of the textile and fashion design duo Timney-Fowler was an art student. Of the important fashion designers from an earlier generation many, such as Jean Muir and Zandra Rhodes, were trained in textile design. So more than couture and designing, and on a par with Westwood's street approach, it is the fine arts and textiles that call the tune in British fashion design.

Besides this more rebellious element, however, fashion in Britain is represented by a more classical 'thoroughbred look' that has percolated through by way of designers like Victor Edelstein, Bruce Oldfield, Alisdair Blair, and Jasper Conran – not forgetting the custom of the likes of Princess Diana. New, enterprising shop owners like Paul Smith, who offers classical outfits with an up-to-date look, are beginning to give the entire fashion area a broader basis. For one of the threats to British fashion is indeed the presence of too many extremes, and the absence of anything substantial in-between. The designer Rifat Ozbek has hit the nail on the head: 'London

TEXTILE DESIGN FOR ARA TIE CO., JAPAN, 1988
Hilde Smith

sensation in the early eighties. Westwood turned out to be the driving force behind it, ever able to stimulate it anew. According to McDermott she is also the originator of another major British contribution to fashion, a cut 'in the round rather than in the flat.'[11] For Suzy Menkes, fashion critic of the *Herald Tribune*, this has given Britain a group of 'New Wave Tailors' which includes Jasper Conran, John Galliano, and John Richmond.[12]

She explains all these innovations, leaving aside the question of

144

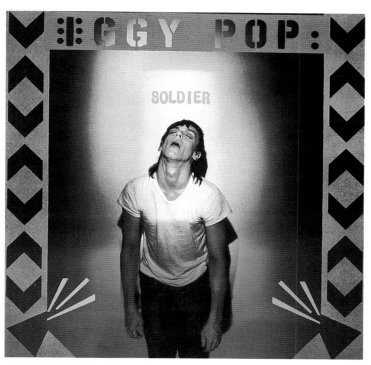

RECORD SLEEVE FOR IGGY POP
Alex McDowell/Rocking Russian
In his use of symbols and emblems, Alex McDowell
influenced Neville Brody's work

FOR THE GLOVE RECORD SLEEVE
Alex McDowell/Rocking Russian

should always be young. That's why everyone comes here and always will. You can't turn London into Milan. I tried to do the suits and the clean look but they don't buy from us when they have Calvin Klein and Giorgio Armani. They want fun.'[14]

Fun is both the strength and weakness of British fashion, the more so because it lacks a well-founded structure to allow fashion to mature. In the sixties the clothing companies, with goods of an exceptionally high quality, began to bow out of the market because of the monopoly of giant retailers like Marks & Spencer. These dominated the market, and made the clothing companies dependent on them with their vast orders, depriving the latter of the need for innovation. Leaving aside small firms producing handmade outfits and shirts for the upper ten, there was little left in the way of craftsmanship. In Galliano's words: 'English factories are only

BOY GEORGE POSTER, 1987
Malcolm Garrett

interested in making 50 p T-shirts. The quality at Indian and Turkish sweatshops is hopeless.'[15] Jasper Conran complains of manufacturers both of textiles and in general who wish to remain outside the fashion industry.[16] But the designers themselves are equally to blame when it comes to being unbusinesslike and unprofessional. Collections and orders are frequently late, and a sense of reality often sadly lacking.

In addition, complaints are rife – according to Nicholas Coleridge, author of *The Fashion Conspiracy* – about the women among British customers, who do not invest in expensive clothes and vanity in general. Indeed London can boast more well-dressed men than women. The difference between British culture and that of more southern countries comes into it too. There is less grandeur, less *joie de vivre;* it is more economical, more respectable, more puritanical; there is no desire to be 'on show'. This is where British design reveals a paradox, for are not the love of dressing up and the sense of show and theatre so much a part of British culture – the very elements that keep presenting new possibilities in fashion?

And yet there are signs, too, that British fashion has outgrown the 'fun' stage. So the oil tycoon Peder Bertelsen is financially supporting many young British fashion designers, thus allowing the innovative tendencies to continue. The internationalising of British culture and a growing spending power have kindled an interest in fashion amongst younger women. What is certain is that the wealth of ideas fashion has to offer can be found in many other, related areas.

Music

Besides fashion, it is music that in Britain constitutes one great melting-pot of ideas uniting people and branches of culture. With his group, the performance artist Bruce McLean presented his ideas in a musical form as early as 1971 under the name Nice Style – The World's First Pose Band. For him music was a medium.[17] The Sex Pistols had their clothes made by Vivienne Westwood; and David Bowie popularised Punk with his bizarre outfits and hairstyles. Westwood's *Pirate* collection and Galliano's *Les Incroyables*, with their

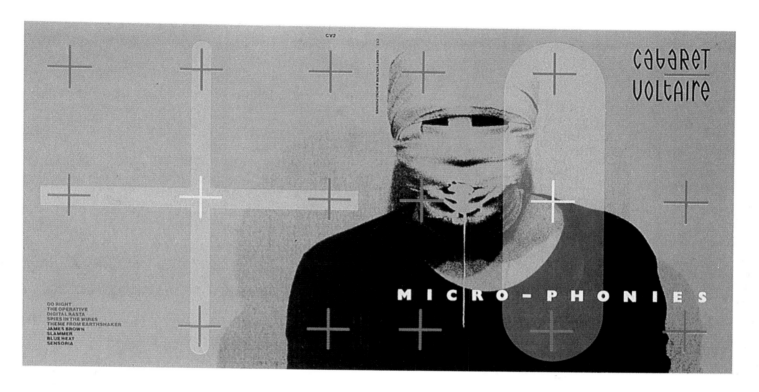

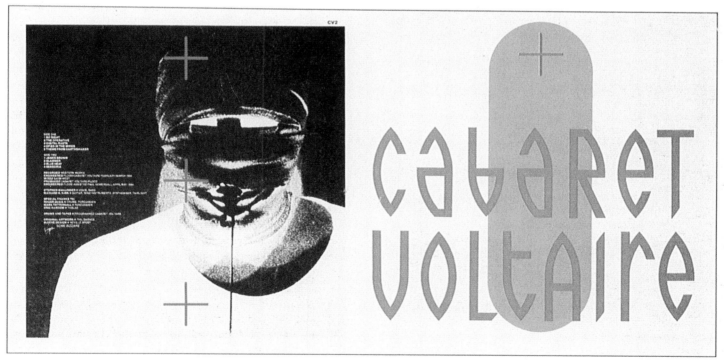

SOME BIZARRE MICROPHONIÉS, COVER AND INNER SLEEVE, 1984
Neville Brody, Virgin Records
We were trying to work against the kind of contived and grandiose imagery

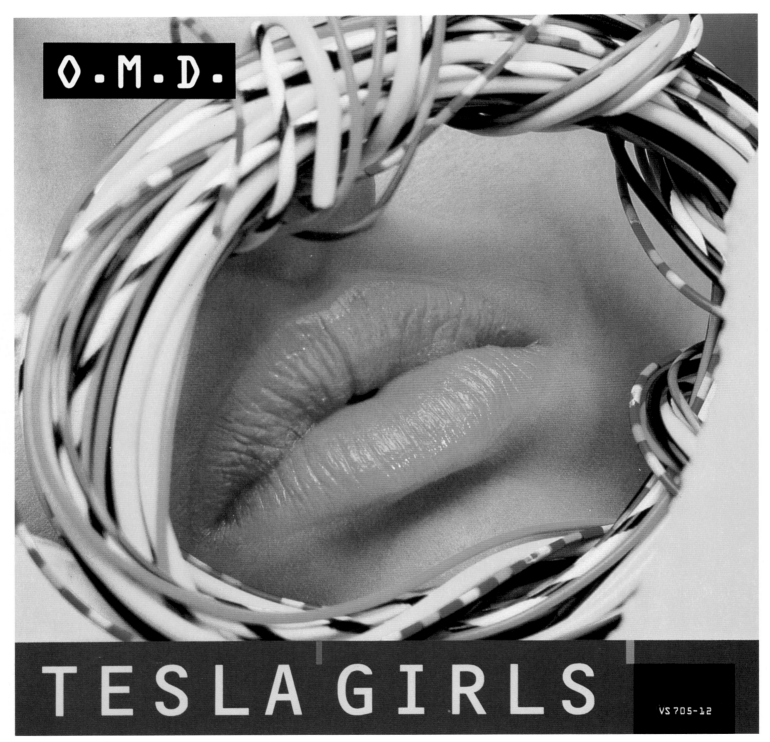

TESLA GIRLS, RECORD SLEEVE,
ORCHESTRAL MANOEUVRES IN THE DARK, 1984
Peter Saville Associates/Trevor Key

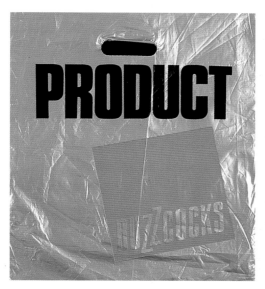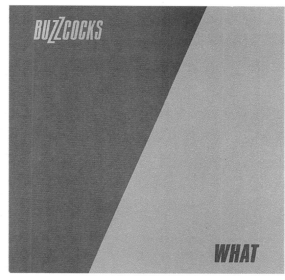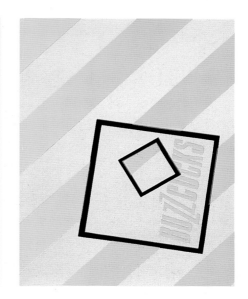

GRAPHICS FOR THE BUZZCOCKS, 1978
Malcolm Garrett

back-to-the-eighteenth-century look, were seized on by the New Romantics, of which Adam Ant was perhaps the most important musical representative. With unusual titles like 'Cat in a Hat takes a Numble with a Techno Fish' by Bodymap in 1984, and their use of dancers, most fashion shows seem more like large-scale stage productions. The pop singer Boy George introduced a new line of fashion to the market. And so the list goes on.

Pop stars have become the trend-setting idols, as film stars once were. Consequently, building up the right image is an essential factor in the music industry, where music has long ceased to be the sole ingredient. Then again, graphic design and the fine arts together with fashion share much common ground with music. Many musicians come from art schools and take a great interest in style. The LP *Sergeant Pepper's Lonely Hearts Club Band* by the Beatles was already

celebrated in 1967 for its sleeve, designed by the artists Peter Blake and Robert Fraser. Richard Hamilton gave a subsequent double LP of theirs an all-white sleeve, while Heinz Edelmann designed that of *Yellow Submarine*. Groups like Pink Floyd and Yes also brought in eminent illustrators and photographers for their record sleeves. To this tradition the Sex Pistols added a sequel. Aided by the simplest of means, Jamie Reid made for them 'low-tech' sleeves that scored an immediate success. Alex McDowell, then a student and now a director of pop videos, began his career in music. His graphic design practice Rocking Russian worked for Iggy Pop amongst others, and in its use of symbols and emblems influenced the work of Neville Brody. The graphic designers Peter Saville, Barney Bubbles, and Malcolm Garrett were others who found success by way of record sleeves. Of this Garrett says: 'We had just left school, were

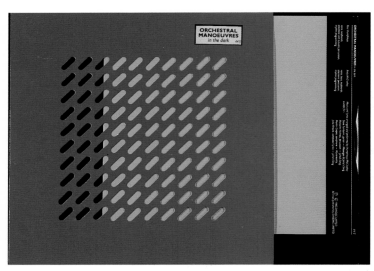

THE DARK ALBUM, RECORD SLEEVE,
ORCHESTRAL MANOEUVRES IN THE DARK, 1981
Peter Saville/Ben Kelly

very naive, and so we just got stuck into it.'[18] A whole new generation of graphic designers appeared in the wake of punk music and prospered not least because of the success of the punk groups. Their common interest was anarchy, the need to break all the rules, or simply ignore them. 'We don't break rules . . . we don't know what the rules are,' insists the graphics duo Designers Republic.[19] 'It was such a low period and we just felt forced to actually go and provoke people as much as possible,' explains Chris Watson of Cabaret Voltaire, a pop group begun in 1973.[20] The graphic designer Neville Brody says: 'We were trying to work against the kind of contrived and grandiose imagery that was signified on Ultravox sleeves, for example, seeking to engage an intuitive reaction that followed on from our own feelings about a sleeve's imagery.'[21] So here, taking many different forms, was a reaction against the

existing order, as much amongst artists as amongst musicians and graphic designers. Brody says the change in the look of record sleeves was partly thanks to the idea then current that music and its content are more important than the personalities of the pop stars themselves. Musicians themselves began exercising a greater influence on their presentation. But Brody also points out that it was the very commerciality of the mass culture of Pop Art that paved the way for a reaction in the form of anti-commercial, unpolished imagery.[22] This aspect was brought to the fore by the arrival of a host of small, independent record companies and design offices.

But, as is to be expected in our society, 'anti' turned into 'pro' and the non-commercial into the commercial, to be wrapped up and turned into a money-spinner by the establishment. The record industry, whose sales took a deep plunge around 1980, had to own up to the fact that the anti element and the abusive character of the punk bands in fact constituted the secret of their success. They had no choice but to believe in it and to accept the new trend. 'The success made them worried about their own position and they had to allow the new bands more freedom,' says Garrett.[23] Many record companies closed down their own art departments and welcomed the young designers to their ranks.

Magazines

Nor did it stop at record sleeves. The magazine market has also learned during the last eight years the meaning of the word 'design'. Between 1975 and 1985 the number of magazines increased by a third, and in 1988 there are more than 3000 in Britain.[24] In this burgeoning market the magazines *i-D* (instant Design) and *The Face*, both aimed at young people and in circulation from 1980, occupy an important position.

With *i-D*, launched by Terry Jones and with its roots in punk fashion, the graphic street style took its place in the commercial scene. The first issue still had the form of a 'fanzine' with thirty black and white sheets stapled together in a glossy cover. In 1986 the circulation had grown to 45 000, yet the DIY look remained.[25] In its hand-typed articles, its lack of grids or basic layout, and its juxtaposition of components pasted together by eye alone, the designers, Terry Jones and Alex McDowell, were mirroring the contents of *i-D*. As Terry Jones says: 'I wanted to get the concept over that we don't lay down the rules about what you wear, the idea of 'in-out' fashion.'[26] Its readers were given a tough time of it, being obliged to make what they could of its layout and typography. 'We're interested in exploring the bounds of illegibility,' explained Jones.[27] Its aesthetic chaos was quickly latched on to by the advertising world and by other magazines.

In contrast with the fashion-based *i-D*, *The Face* came from the music scene. It was set up as a music magazine by Nick Logan, who before that had worked for another, *Smash Hits*. Ultimately it was the intention to expand into a general magazine for young people. For the graphic designer Neville Brody it was his work for *The Face* that rocketed him to fame. He gave it a look very much its own, with new letter types treated in an individual way. In addition *The Face* stood out from the rest through its layout, which made use of large photographs facing pages of print that were full of witty and powerful graphic symbols. 'I wanted every spread you opened to be a poster.

COVER FOR THE FACE, 1985
Neville Brody

PAGE SPREAD FROM THE FACE, 1985
Neville Brody, I wanted every spread to look like a poster

I wanted to surprise people and maintain a rhythm that was based on a different set of elements. I felt that if you opened a page that stopped you in your tracks, then you would want to read on.'[28]

The 'Brody look' of *The Face* began to proliferate in the newspaper kiosks; not only because it was assiduously copied by others, but also because Brody himself went on to work for magazines like *The New Socialist, City Limits*, and *Arena*. Here, too, the influence on advertising was so great that at one time it was virtually impossible to separate the advertisements from the articles.

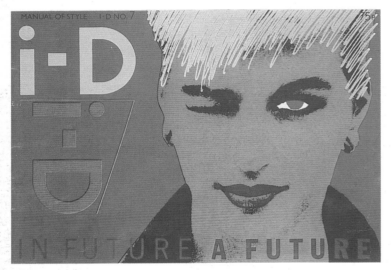

COVER OF I-D FIVE-YEAR ANNIVERSARY ISSUE, 1985
Terry Jones
DIY look

Arena shows this most clearly.

In fashion, music, and graphic design, British youth has demonstrated quite clearly its ability to ditch tradition entirely, and replace it with ideas of its own. In this the streetside rebellion complements that launched by the art schools. Now is the time to evaluate these achievements and follow them up. At the time of writing there is a large group of young graphic designers that shows a desire to return to the rules and to the modernist typographical tradition. Anarchy, as I see it, keeps the experimental side alive if nothing else, and ensures a variety of approaches and plenty of discussion. Although some of this energy will be swallowed up by the giant commercial structures of the media, they in turn will inspire the other, hitherto ultraconservative clients to take a more adventurous line.

Furthermore, these magazines were disheartening to the clients of advertising agencies, who, suspecting they were behind the times, sought a more youth culture-orientated look.

Many of the graphic innovations in these periodicals date back to a tradition of 'underground' magazines that began in the sixties and is still around today. In addition, technology in the form of computer-operated typesetting made it possible to distort the type, alter the width of columns, and assemble the magazine at the computer keyboard. Finally, we may well wonder if these magazines were so revolutionary after all. The eclecticism of juxtaposed images is certainly no British invention, having been used at an earlier date in the Netherlands. Nor is breaking the rules a quality in its own right. Moreover, Brody's designing includes unmistakably classical elements, and a striving to bring each page to a state of repose –

BOY BOY

BIBLE

i-D

BUY BOY

GREETINGS FROM LONDON

THE FACE

VOLUME 2 No 3 DECEMBER 1988 £1.30 @ US $3.75

HOUSE POST-ACID:
THE NEW CLUB SOUND

CHET BAKER
BY BRUCE WEBER

WALTON:
POST-MODERN

BOY

Nowhere are the boundaries so blurred and the mutual cross-fertilisation of myriad cultural areas so great, however, as in the medium that has become so crucial to youth culture, the pop music video. Here music, the visual arts, film, photography, graphic design, and advertising are brought together, as are the avant garde and the commercial. For while the pop video is meant to get music as a product across to the public, it has become a product in its own right, and, increasingly, of greater importance than the music itself. Apart from pop videos this chapter also deals with British advertising. Both media enjoy a vigorous interaction with design, graphic and otherwise, and have been crucial in establishing a style-based, visual culture. Also, both are an extension of the street and similar sources of inspiration.

If it moves, they will watch it

The pop video business unifies a remarkable amount of British talent. Kevin Godley and Lol Creme, both ex-art students and former members of the pop group 10CC, have been responsible for the most way-out pop videos; the graphic designer and art director Alex

McDowell emerged as a pop video director; and also film-makers like Steve Barron and Julian Temple have left their mark on the medium. Moreover, it is one of the most rapidly expanding sectors in Britain. In 1985 the field of television manufacture expanded by 25%, and pop videos together with videograms brought in between 20 and 30 million pounds.[1]

Where the pop video originated is a matter of dispute. As an art form it has an affinity with opera, although the object character dominates the performing side in the pop video. Also, it reveals visual parallels with the art films of the twenties and thirties. On a more mundane level, it may have started when American groups began sending films to television programmes instead of appearing.[2] Whatever the case, it was Andy Warhol who understood it best when he said: 'If it moves, they will watch it.'[3] He also anticipated the idea of the artist being more important than art. His mentality and his films were to help the birth of the pop video. However, the first genuine (and, I might add, British) pop video, *Bohemian Rhapsody* from 1975, was directed by Bruce Gowers and produced by John Roseman for the group Queen. It was clearly made with the commercial promotion of the music in mind, and was more than just a registering of a performance. After being shown on BBC's *Top Of*

COMMERCIAL FOR LEVI'S, 1985
Bartle Bogle Hegarthy art director, John Hegarthy, copywriter, Barbara Nokes, director, Roger Lyons, producer, Noel Bennett

SLEDGEHAMMER POP VIDEO
Peter Gabriel, photographer Armando Gallo

The Pops the single became a bestseller for three months.

In the years that followed, the music industry in the shape of the pop video took television by storm, and with pop videos as staple diet more and more pop music programmes were televised. Furthermore, pop videos seem also to be a last-ditch attempt to win back the record-buying public, which during the last years has been dwindling at an alarming rate.

Promo or advert?

In its brevity the pop video has a greater affinity with the television commercial than with film, but differs vastly from it in other respects. Three to six minutes is too short to constitute a story, but too long to be a commercial. The director Alex McDowell calls the pop video 'a

commercial shown as entertainment.'[4] Lol Creme is even for excluding every narrative element. 'The important thing in making a video is to create an atmosphere rather than tell a story. Musicians don't make convincing actors so you need to film something which complements the music.'[5]

In general, however, pop videos are put together according to a well-tried formula: performing musicians for a third of the time, glamour girls, a smattering of sex, a dash of violence, lots of effects and movement, and every three seconds a change of shot. Everything has to be recorded in the extremely short space of a few days. This regimented production process and the commercial pressures leave little room for innovation. Eight years ago one could make a video for 4 000 pounds; now the average budget is five times as much, and for 100 000 pounds a video director can really go to town, although the days of really big budget videos are over.[6]

Experiments and business

In the beginning, relates McDowell, the video industry was set up by entrepreneurs and marketing men rather than film-makers.[7] At the same time however, at the close of the seventies groups like the Human League and Cabaret Voltaire started revitalising the medium through their experiments with film and video. The video boom was on its way.

Hipgnosis, an office designing record sleeves, set up the Greenback subsidiary to handle video and advertising. The *enfants terribles* of the British feature film, Steve and Siobhan Barron, followed in 1978 with Limelight, a company that would later spawn so many major video directors. At this time, too, the photographer Anton Corbijn and the musicians Godley and Creme moved into pop video production. Together with film directors like Russell Mulcahey and Julien Temple, and through the contribution of musicians like David Bowie, they breathed new life into the medium.
Bowie, because of his exceptional mimical talents, makes the perfect video star. His video's, directed by David Mallett and Julien Temple,

156

**SET DESIGN FOR THE VIDEO WHEN ALLS WELL,
EVERYTHING BUT THE GIRL, 1985**
Alex McDowell, director Tim Pope

RED GUITAR POP VIDEO FOR DAVID SYLVIAN, 1984
director, Anton Corbijn, producer, Luc Roeg, camera, Dennis Crossan,
produced by Aldabra Ltd.

DR. MABUSE POP VIDEO, PROPAGANDA, 1984
director, Anton Corbijn, producer, Nikki Picasso
camera, Sid MacCarthy, produced by Aldabra Ltd.
An all black-and-white video

are about alienation, loss of identity, and the artist as role-player. He is the key figure of the so-called New Romantics, musicians with an aptitude for theatre and stardom, like Boy George, The Skids, Adam Ant, Spandau Ballet, and Ultravox. This wave was soon followed by groups who gave the director more leeway, such as Duran Duran and The Police.

'Of course you're being paid to make the group look better, but some of these groups are so naive that they have no idea of what's going on anyway. That gives you the room to do things that won't give you sleepless nights.'[8] In *Poison Arrow* by the group ABC, Temple reversed the male chauvinistic attitude towards women common to most pop videos, by instead having the star of the video humiliated by a woman. Anton Corbijn feels that '. . . in all honesty I

don't believe that the majority of pop singers have particularly great artistic ambitions. They just get what they want. In the case of most groups the videos show them as they really are. Sometimes the pop videos outshine the groups. But mostly the groups get what they deserve.'[9]

So the outstanding video is born when the director enjoys a measure of freedom, and when the musicians have definite creative ideas themselves. Take Peter Gabriel's *Sledgehammer*, directed by Stephen Johnson, which in 1986 broke new ground through the different types of animation used in it. But pop videos produced by the musicians themselves can be relied on for innovative qualities too. By making films in which existing television-images were alienated, Cabaret Voltaire with director Peter Care anticipated the collage-like

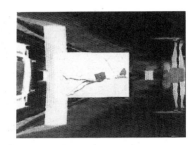

LEGS POP VIDEO
The Art of Noise

scratch technique used today. Other outstanding pop videos include *Once in a Lifetime* by Talking Heads (1980), *Hyperactive* by Thomas Dolby (1984), *Cry* by Godley and Creme (1986), and *Legs* by The Art of Noise (1986).

Melting pot

The individual cases aside, how is it that the British pop video has attained such a high level? In the first place, according to McDowell, because the directors derived not from the TV commercial, as was the case in America, but from the art schools.[10] For instance, in 1975 the Royal College of Art set up a Department of Environmental Media, known as the 'avant garde ghetto', where boundaries between

art disciplines played no role, and where performance art, video, and film were practised.

The British pop video also has roots in the film tradition (including the low-budget 'underground' film), which means both capable directors and the chance to experiment. There are, besides, considerable mutual contacts between graphic designers, musicians, photographers, and the advertising world. The exchange of ideas within this relatively small circle is more rapid than it is in, say, America. As Godley and Creme put it, 'because the country [America] is so big, it takes longer for new ideas to percolate through the system.'[11] In their opinion America is several years behind Britain in this respect, also because Americans are not particularly receptive to conceptual 'style' videos.[12] However, the Americans do have bigger budgets and more professional means, although McDowell points out that British producers and camera crews are now more at home in the field of pop videos than they were, and that this medium is steadily acquiring some sort of structure.[13] Peter York states that apart from music and the art schools, one of the cornerstones of the pop video is Britain's advertising culture.[14] It is the conceptual approach of advertising that has made its mark here.

On top of this, Britain is leading in the field of computer graphics (animation), bringing it to a higher artistic and technological level than anywhere else in the world. Finally, the influence of the independent television station Channel Four should not be underestimated. With its enlightened commission policy it has proved

SENSORIA POP VIDEO, CABARET VOLTAIRE
director, Peter Care

160

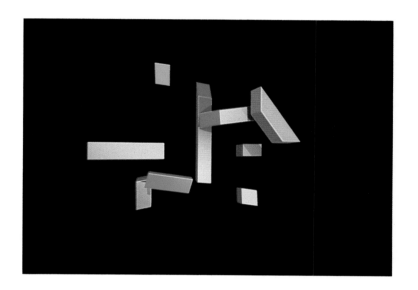
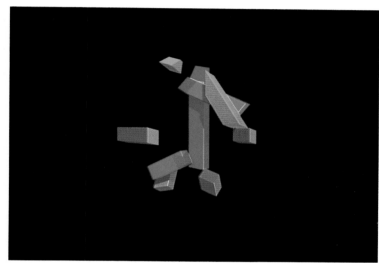
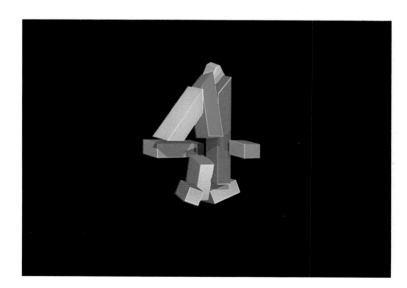
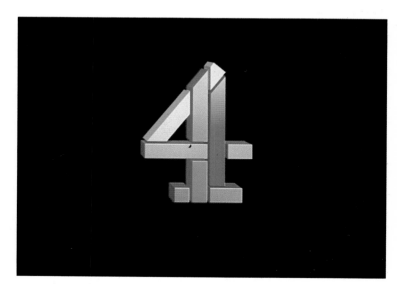

CORPORATE IDENTITY FOR CHANNEL FOUR, 1982
director, Martin Lambie-Nairn design and production, Robinson Lambie-Nairn Ltd.,
computer animation, Bo Gehring Aviation, Los Angeles
editor, John Cary

**GRAPHIC DEVICE TO INTRODUCE A
COMMERCIAL BREAK FOR ANGLIA TELEVISION**
*creative director, Martin Lambie-Nairn director, Philip Dupee,
designer, Derek Hayes, animation, Animation City,
design and production, Robinson Lambie-Nairn Ltd.,
paintbox, Harry & Encore, CAL Video Graphics*

THERE

IS ONLY ONE

HARRODS.

————

THERE

IS ONLY ONE

SALE.

COMMENCES JULY 8TH.

SALES CAMPAIGN FOR HARROD'S, 1987-88
Leagas Delaney, art director, Steve Dunn, copywriter Tim Delaney,
photographer, Daniel Jouanneau, typography, Steve Dunn

a shot in the arm for animation, TV graphics, and the video field. The two-way contact between media has meant that the boundaries between them are dissolving. Thus many video directors are also making TV commercials, while in turn the pop video has influenced television programmes, the visual arts, and feature films.
The difference between reality, show, and advertising is becoming less and less distinct.

Images for sale

During the last ten years advertising has become big business in Britain. London is, outside America, the world's biggest advertising centre, and everyone seems to be involved, up to and including political parties and the government. In television programmes it is the subject of discussion, and newspaper columns are increasingly full of it. *The Sunday Times* recently began a special marketing and advertising supplement.

Saatchi & Saatchi, who began so modestly in 1967, have since graduated to the Times Top 100 Companies. Of the ten biggest advertising agencies in the world, one is British – and this is probably just the beginning of the onslaught.[15] For the tidal wave of fusions and takeovers involving agencies like WPP would seem to be anything but played out. New clients like the government – in 1987

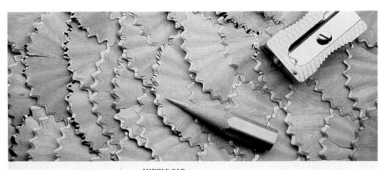

MIDDLE TAR As defined by H.M Government
DANGER: Government Health WARNING: CIGARETTES CAN SERIOUSLY DAMAGE YOUR HEALTH

MIDDLE TAR As defined by H.M Government
Warning: SMOKING CAN CAUSE LUNG CANCER, BRONCHITIS AND OTHER CHEST DISEASES
Health Departments' Chief Medical Officers

ADVERTISEMENTS FOR BENSON AND HEDGES, 1986 & 1987
Collett, Dickenson, Pearce and Partners Ltd., photographers, Kevin Summers,
Richard Mummmery, art directors, Nigel Rose, Graham Fink

with 88 million pounds Britain's second biggest advertiser – the political world, banks, and pension schemes are adding to this growth.[16] And new categories like corporate advertising, geared to increasing or stabilising both share prices and the confidence of investors, are doing likewise. At the same time, the advertised products themselves are changing less and less, because technological progress is overtaking any alterations or improvements with increasing swiftness. Besides, competitors soon adopt these changes themselves. Consequently, products are being sold less and less on rational grounds. The consumer buys the perception of the product, and advertising either alters or perpetuates this.

Advertising, whether 'graphics in the service of commerce', 'the application of creative skills to selling products and ideas', 'commercial art', or 'the business of making images for sale': 'it sells goods and services by turning them into images and dreams.'[17] These days, however, advertising is becoming more and more the product itself.

What makes British advertising so British, and why did London, rather than anywhere else, become its creative centre?

'Labour isn't working' is the legend on a poster depicting a dole queue. Another shows an 'expectant father' asking 'Would you be more careful if it was you that got pregnant?' A third uses the associative image of just the colour gold, with below it a terse government warning against the perils of smoking. This, then, is British advertising – provocative, evocative, refined, associative, subtle, and humorous. The things they are promoting become clear only after a second glance: the Conservative Party, the use of contraceptives, and Benson & Hedges cigarettes. The above campaigns, daring and adventurous, and – above all – adult, were landmarks in the British approach to advertising.

A comparison with America says much about British advertising. In an article in *Design* Jane Lott asserts that advertising in America is more sentimental, as Americans are more used to emotional blackmail, as compared to the British with their more disciplined upbringing. She also brings up one American criticism of British advertising, namely that it is sterile.[18] For American advertising agencies, research is of overriding importance; and the more research, it seems, the more stereotyped the advertisement. Moreover, Americans go for a quite different, much more direct line of attack. Their advertisements are more factual, more 'hard sell',

164

LOW TAR As defined by H.M. Government
Warning: SMOKING CAN CAUSE LUNG CANCER, BRONCHITIS AND OTHER CHEST DISEASES
Health Departments' Chief Medical Officers

LOW TAR As defined by H.M. Government
STOPPING SMOKING REDUCES THE RISK OF SERIOUS DISEASES
Health Departments' Chief Medical Officers

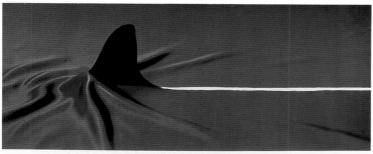

LOW TAR As defined by H.M. Government
Warning: SMOKING CAN CAUSE FATAL DISEASES
Health Departments' Chief Medical Officers

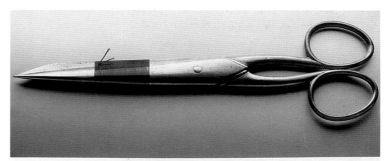

LOW TAR As defined by H.M. Government
Warning: MORE THAN 30,000 PEOPLE DIE EACH YEAR IN THE UK FROM LUNG CANCER
Health Departments' Chief Medical Officers

ADVERTISEMENTS FOR SILK CUT, 1987
Saatchi & Saatchi, art directors, Alan Burles, Jerry Hollens,
Adrian Kemsley, Alexandra Taylor, copywriters, Moira Townsend,
Mike Boles, Mick Petherick photography, Barry Lategan,
Graham Ford, Daniel Jouanneau

**CAMPAIGN AGAINST THE ABOLITION
OF THE GREATER LONDON COUNCIL, 1986**
Boase Massimi Pollitt, art director, Peter Gatley, copywriter, John Pallant

ADVERTISEMENT FOR THE HEALTH EDUCATION COUNCIL, 1968
Saatchi & Saatchi art director, Bill Atherton, copywriter, Jeremy Sinclair

and less humorous, whereas the British pursue a subtler, more seductive approach. According to the American art director Carl Hixon, the British are masters of the double meaning. While the words of a beer commercial are saying that it tastes good, refreshes, or is low in calories, the visual message, according to him, is that it 'gets you laid, gives you peer status, helps you master situations.'[19] 'In America', says the ex-director of *Campaign* advertising magazine, Bernard Barnett, 'advertising is business-business, here it's show business.'[20] The British attitude to selling is not a direct one; this approach they find embarrassing. In general they are not that fond of making money and conducting business in the first place, let alone talking about it openly.

As well as being subtle and indirect British advertising is also more pleasing. For Stephen Bayley it is the television commercial that best exhibits this quality.[21] As viewers have a choice between channels with and without commercials they would simply switch elsewhere, he maintains, if confronted with irritating or aggressive commercials. The British TV commercial did not derive from radio advertising, as it did in the States. It is more a smaller version of the film commercial, which is why, besides being pleasing, it also has a more narrative character.

Could this agreeable quality of the TV commercial have some connection with British film directors, who are able to create such beautiful, aesthetic images *(Brideshead Revisited, Chariots of Fire, A Room with a View)*? The British film industry is if nothing else a 'pool' of capable professionals whose talents are channelled during lean periods into making commercials. In addition, the BBC, with its

tradition of non-commercial programmes of a high educational and cultural standard, serves as a place of apprenticeship for many students and film-makers.

The growth of television as a medium – commercial television hit Britain in 1955 – might have strengthened the 'Britishness' of the British advertisement. In any case, television is by its very nature better suited to images and emotions than to factual information. The rise of the TV commercial has encouraged the abandoning of rational, product-directed advertising. This seems to have filtered

CAMPAIGN FOR THE CONSERVATIVE PARTY, 1979
Saatchi & Saatchi art director, Martyn Walsh, copywriter, Andrew Rutherford

ADVERTISEMENT FOR AUDI, 1988
Bartle Bogle Hegarthy art director, John Gorse, copyriter, Nick Worthington,
photography, Kevin Summers

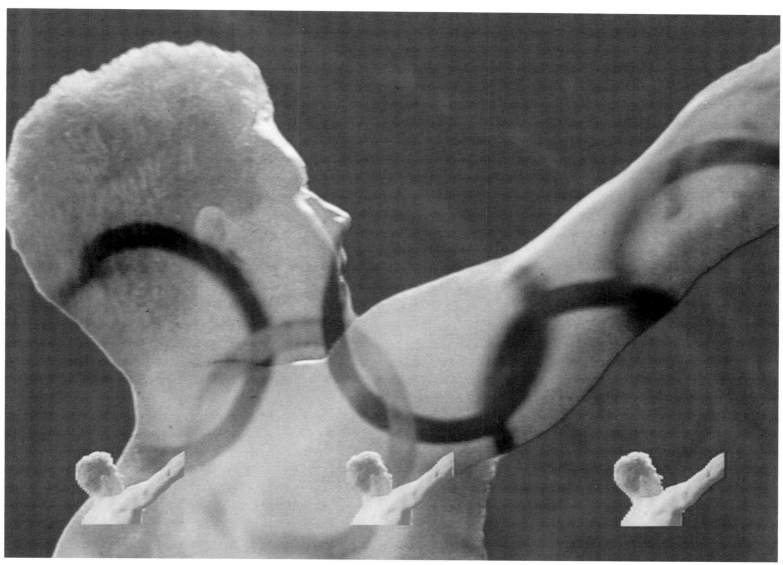

TRAILER FOR THE OLYMPIC GAMES, 1988
designed by Madelaine MacGregor at Channel 4 and produced at CAL Video Graphics
by Terry Hylton and Rob Harvey

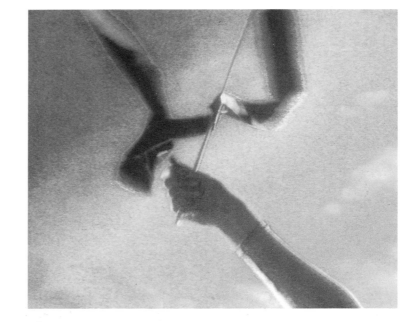

TRAILER FOR THE OLYMPIC GAMES, 1988
designed by Glenn Carwithen for the BBC,
produced by Cell Animation

through to industry as well. According to Chris Edwards, publicity agent for Peugeot: 'We are growing in awareness and challenging competition that has been around for a long time by offering excitement and style. It's not necessarily essential to see all of the car in a commercial – you no longer have to spell it out. That way it becomes more memorable.'[22] In an increasing number of British advertisements there are no brand names or products to be seen, only intriguing images that may tease the brain for days with the question 'What is being advertised?' The understatement is gaining ground.

In a short space of time, television advertising has undergone a process of refinement. 'When I started doing television at Saatchi's', relates John Hegarthy who in 1982 co-founded the Bartle Bogle Hegarthy agency, 'the only people who knew about it were the Americans or heads of TV who had often moved from broadcasting.'[23] Among other things, he was responsible for the celebrated Levi's laundrette commercial with its strong fifties feel, and the 'Vorsprung durch Technik' campaign for Audi. Most BBH commercials are based on a story and avoid visual effects and fuss. At the beginning of the eighties the existing offices like Saatchi & Saatchi, Boase Massimi Pollitt, and Collett Dickenson Pearce were augmented by new ones continuing the creative tendencies, such as BBH, WCRS, Abbott Mead Vickers, and Gold Greenless Trott.

17th century silver mirror. The Victoria & Albert Museum. Two minutes from South Kensington tube.

All right, the mirror's seen better days but the currant buns are very tasty.

V&A An ace caff with quite a nice museum attached.

SAATCHI'S CAMPAIGN FOR THE VICTORIA AND ALBERT MUSEUM
Design and advertising are becoming ever more closely related

On the whole British advertisements are much more conceptual than elsewhere. The graphic designer Gert Dumbar suspects this has something to do with the visual quality of British thinking, based on a concept. 'They [the British] think more in visual than in abstract terms. Then again, there is the incredible subtlety and flexibility of the English language. The tendency to link image and language is very strong.'[24] He also draws attention to the fact that the British agencies' clients allow more in their advertisements than is the case in other countries. In his book *The Want Makers* Eric Clark says that the British advertising world itself is showing more scepticism as to the power of advertising.[25] Then there is the D&AD – in the person of its chairman, Edward Booth-Clibborn, who has been an untiring promoter of creativity in British visual communication – which has done much to build up the image of British advertising as the best in the world.

But what I see as the most important factor, is once again the open structure of the British advertising world, which admits first-rate young talent with no regard to education or background. And it is working class talent which enjoys unlimited space here. So too does the creative talent from the art schools. The art director Derrick Hass, originally a graphic designer, says: 'Advertising, of course, was always looked down on slightly by designers for its washing powder connotations but that started to change with cigarette advertising . . . where you had to find exciting graphic solutions, had to resolve the problem of not being able to say anything.'[26] Whatever else, young talent in the advertising world has managed to avoid contamination by ideas about design-pureness or other weighty traditions.

CONCLUSION

The identity of British design is no easy thing to pin down. The more one looks at British design, the more difficult it becomes to put it under one heading. Fashionable tendencies intermingle with tradition, visual styles from elsewhere are quickly absorbed, and most design areas testify to a great diversity. Influences come from the street, from tradition, from both modernism and classicism. Seen as a whole, British design is a many-faceted affair. There is little question of a single British identity, in visual terms, that holds true for all design sectors. Any such *leitmotiv* is elusive indeed.

Take the craft ideal, for instance, a tradition that in the United Kingdom is still very much in evidence. This can be attributed largely to the British predilection for nature, a weakness for the amateur, and a taste for individualism. But we should not forget a love of materials, the narrative, literary side of British culture, and the age-old importance attached to skilled workmanship. The craft mentality has long been the decisive force behind British design giving it its practicality, its 'doing-as-designing'. British arts and crafts proved itself capable of self-renewal, just because of this very continuity and its isolated, introverted position. This continuity and a strong ideological basis have given British arts and crafts its identity. The narrative aspect, the decorative, linear elements, and a love of

materials have been ever-present in the British craft movement. Its aloof position and scepticism towards industry emerged as a weakness at those times when faith in industry dominated culture, and as a strength at moments when industrial values were faced with a crisis, as in the nineteenth century – or today. Now in particular, British craft-based perspectives seem able to offer new inroads for industry. Up till now, however, these qualities have been tapped mainly by non-British manufacturers.

The British industrial mass product, on the other hand, is far less individual. There is little about it that stands out, and it testifies to a dearth of feeling for the plastic and three-dimensional; as in domestic appliances, for instance. It neither takes chances, by and large, nor does it break away radically from established patterns. The decorative and domestic prevail, rather than structural or formative aspects, at the risk of lapsing into anecdote. It lacks the grand statement. The radios of Ekco and Murphy, illustrated in chapter one, are for me unsurpassed in this respect. The way in which some designers try to find new forms for these seems forced; the proportions are awkward, and they clearly evoke the image familiar to us from many British films: the sombre thirties and forties, utility clothes, the middle-class family in the living room. At its worst, the average British product design is more servile and superficial than adventurous or shocking. At its best it is well-balanced, subtle, and respectable.

The more technologically orientated industries, on the other hand, have managed to come up with exceptional products, aircraft, cars, engines, and suchlike. There has been a flood of ingenious and spectacular inventions: people like Moulton, Issigonis, and Sinclair have been responsible for a string of classics. In this the tradition of individualism and the amateur has shown itself an essential prerequisite.

As for British graphic design, its characteristics include classicism, symmetry, and structure. It is well-balanced, explicit, and uncomplicated in its approach; pragmatic, even. The British typographical tradition of books and love of the letter is at the root of this. In British graphic design a modernistic, more dynamic approach to typography, such as that of Germany or the Netherlands, is nowhere to be found. So although Neville Brody did create new typefaces for the magazine *The Face*, he used them in a wholly decorative way; they bear no relation to he treatment of the text in general. Words and images in British graphic design are often two separate entities. This is because, besides typography, graphic design also has roots in the illustration, a tradition that tends more towards the narrative and anecdotal than to structure or abstraction. A noteworthy aspect is the openness to foreign influences, which British graphics assimilates effortlessly. And nor is this a phenomenon of the twenties and thirties either, for today its feelers are once again going out to countries like the Netherlands and America, and to historical styles too. Periods of foreign influence seem to alternate with years when 'neo' styles set the trend, as in the fifties. In addition, the technological changes of recent years have sparked off a great deal of experimentation. And of course graphic design is less limited than other branches in terms of execution. Expensive research or product development are unnecessary, and the commercial risks much smaller. British graphic design comes across as a ragbag of styles and influences – Constructivism; the ad hoc juxtaposition of components; tasteful, classical packaging; sweeping

American-style statements; and a subtle mildness of manner. It is both eclectic and synthetising.

British fashion is many-layered, almost narrative in quality, with romanticism and ruralism its points of reference. Rather than opting for simplicity and classicism British fashion designers prefer a more complicated line and a full-bodied cut. Fashion in Great Britain has more to do with an airy feminity (Conran, Galliano), the Baroque (Ozbek), or noise (Westwood). Then again, the classical and the traditional live on by continually being reworked. So fashion, too, is difficult to describe in terms of one style or tendency.

Adjectives emerging from these observations and common to the above branches of design include narrative, decorative, anecdotal, eclectic and not tending to abstraction; classical, well-balanced, pragmatic, and synthetising. Striking, too, is the constant assimilation of influences from abroad, by way of foreigners who during their stay in Great Britain manage to infiltrate the British design world, for example Ron Arad (Israel), André Dubreuil (France), Floris van den Broecke (Holland), Daniel Weil (Argentina). Openness, tolerance, and a lack of dogmatism are instrumental in generating a pluralism of approaches. If there is a single characteristic and recognisable British style, I for one have yet to come across it.

Structure

Many of the above-mentioned characteristics can, I feel, be traced back to a lack of structure. The romantic individualism of the Arts and Crafts practitioners stood in the way of integration with industry. Mass production was slow in catching on amongst British designers. There have always been few clients willing to encourage new, and thus more risky, undertakings. Firms imbued with a sense of culture, such as Olivetti, Braun, and IBM, are few and far between. Designers trying to gain entrance to the manufacturing industries generally have a hard time doing so. After all, it was the makers of consumer goods (tableware, furniture, domestic appliances) who suffered greatly from the economic crises. And the few who remain feel no real need to take risks. Hence deferential and respectable, with an exception now and again, is about as far as it gets. It is not for nothing that so many British designers are throwing in their lot with foreign manufacturers, or starting production themselves.

Fashion, too, lacks a sturdy basis or a proper working production structure. An enterprising industrial culture has long been conspicuous by its absence. Scientific discoveries and inventions make little headway in terms of commercial application followed by effective marketing. Industry reacts defensively instead of taking preemptive steps, and often lacks a long-term outlook. Amongst the authorities and governmental institutions design has yet to become institutionalised. In graphics, too, British clients give designers little room to move. Innovations and fresh impulses in British design come almost invariably from the fringe areas, like graphic design and designer-makers, or from outsiders. Inventors generally are engineers or self-taught individuals with a sense of form, or people outside the design establishment in some other way.

Status quo

The second major underlying factor is in my opinion the hierarchy of Britain's class society. Refusing to accept, or steering clear of, extremes and conforming to the established order of things (the pragmatic approach); being respectable and not breaking the rules: these are attitudes very much at home in a culture in which maintaining the status quo is the highest good. By and large, British design is not given to powerful statements and shooting straight from the shoulder. Equally, engineers are still having to struggle to shake off their traditionally low status. A multi-disciplinary approach – though developed early on amongst designers – has barely filtered through to the industries. And government institutions seem only open to 'design' as an image-builder. A matter-of-fact, practical approach and taking things in stages have always appealed to British designers more than extremes, whether these be home-grown or from abroad.

Nor do British designers cling to principles or theories. Unlike British architects, who can claim a long tradition of questioning their profession, designers seem less stricken by self-doubt. This could be explained as the consequence of designers having spent too many years trying to get their profession recognised. Nor have they found an industrial structure capable of serving as a basis. As long as one of these two needs remains unsatisfied there could well be no room to stand back and take an objective look at the profession. And if they finally do succeed in putting design on the cultural and economic map, euphoria would probably prevail to begin with. The general British aversion both to intellectuals and abstract thinking comes in here too. Possibly it is these factors which have made it difficult for designers to take a detached look at themselves and their task, trade in the homely for the wordly, and question their commission. As for those who succeeded in this, such as Christopher Dresser and Charles Rennie Mackintosh, it was probably due to their outstanding individual capacities. But the lack of dogma or structure makes for a greater toleration and freedom as well.

Therefore one cannot say there are no extremes in British design. The outsiders, to be found in fashion and amongst the designer-makers and inventors, time and again add spice to British design. The class structure, status quo, and an avoidance of emotions give rise to a veritable cauldron of extreme reactions, brimful with energy and boiling over on occasions. But these extremes are for this reason short-lived. Punk could never have arisen in a more moderate, levelled down, welfare state like Sweden or the Netherlands. But, if it were to do so, it would not be so apolitical and superficial (i.e. it would not leave the existing order undisturbed). Because this protest was chiefly visual and symbolic, it could easily be appropriated by commercialism. Furthermore, we may well ask just how extreme such countercurrents really are, and how heavily they lean on developments elsewhere, as is the case with graphic design. Moreover, breaking the rules and elevating individual originality was something that occupied young designers in other countries as well. Design ideologies until recently providing certainty, broke down and set a new zero level in the eighties. It is striking also that extremes occur chiefly where they are meant to occur, such as in fashion, music, and the media. Transience and rapid obsolescence are second nature to these areas.

At all events such extremes always seek a means of expression beyond existing channels. Tradition with all its deep-seated structures and prejudices, or rather the lack of tradition, is the cause of the acceptance of this creative aggression. For it is chiefly the non-traditional sectors, unencumbered by a past, which assimilate them. Tradition and innovation, hierarchy and anarchy – in British design each enables the other to exist.

Whenever the burden of the past is absent, or has been jettisoned, there suddenly seems much more room for all manner of new utterances. Design can flourish providing it comes across as commercial and fashionable. When dependent on research and industry, or related to social values, its acceptance is a far more laborious affair. Consequently ephemeral products, packaging, posters, interiors, and style constitute the groundwork for the professionalising of design in Great Britain. Advertising and P.R. consciousness have played a major role here. In this respect I consider the British advertisement to be most representative of the qualities I praise in British design: ironic, humorous, understated, adult, subversive, provocative, visual, ephemeral, and powerful.

The capacities in the fields of advertising, corporate identity, image, and commerce are being strengthened further by Prime Minister Thatcher's 'enterprise culture'. Packaging and selling products are better suited to British designers than are the technological and structural aspects. This ability ties in with the current British industrial élan borne aloft largely by the younger businesses and by a no-nonsense commercial approach. The openness of British society is another vitally important aspect. It is often foreigners who introduce change to the ranks of British design. But British culture itself has become much more international in recent years too.

Having become more professional and more international, coupled with a receptiveness to ideas, gives British design a

tremendous advantage over that of other countries, and makes it well-equipped for 1992. I can only hope that there is still room for subversion and critical alternatives; that the basis broadens and becomes stronger, that 'design' as hype does not mean the end of design proper – and perhaps above all that all the hedonism and the emphasis on money will be balanced by the British propensity for putting things into perspective.

NOTES

Chapter one: The Britishness of British Design

1. quoted MacCarthy 1982, p. 27/note 10.
2. quoted Pevsner 1986, p. 80/note 47.
3. Idem.
4. Historian Alan Macfarlane gives as hallmarks of a revolution newness and suddenness accompanied by violence, unavoidable when overthrowing existing conditions. He goes on to discuss the wide influence of these changes, which occur at many levels of society. Macfarlane 1987.
5. Crick 1988.
6. 'Wanderings in the Crystal Palace', *The Art Journal*, (1851), May, p. 180.
7. According to Pevsner so-called facade architecture was born in the United Kingdom because this country was the first to separate interior and exterior, as in St. Pancras Station of Sir George Gilbert Scott. Pevsner 1986.
8. quoted Naylor 1971, p. 19.
9. quoted MacCarthy 1982, p. 23/note 4.
10. Huygen 1985, p. 22.
11. Braidwood 1986.
12. Olins 1986.
13. Sampson 1982.
14. Thackara 1988, p. 34.
15. quoted Coleridge 1988, p. 132.
16. cat. *National Characteristics in Design*, London, (Boilerhouse), 1985, np.

17. Huygen 1985, p. 22.
18. Pevsner 1986.
19. Macfarlane 1978 and 1987.
20. Marquand 1988.
21. Thompson 1977.
22. Thackara 1988, p. 163.

Chapter two: England as the Garden

1. They thoroughly investigated three widely dissimilar counties during the period between 1540 and 1880 and discovered a proportionally low number of manufacturers among the upper class. Between 1840 and 1879, for example, of a total of 3200 landowners less than fifty self-made men could be found who at their deaths left large landed estates. Stone 1986.
2. Idem, p. 145.
3. Idem, p. 184.
4. Nairn 1988.
5. Stone asserts that the differences in status in British society were dominated by the concept of the gentleman. The notion of the gentleman was defined during the Renaissance, not according to birth or profession, but to manners. The character of the gentleman is by definition that of a man of leisure. Stone 1986.

6. Idem, p. 18.
7. quoted Arnstein 1973, p. 234.
8. Donald Horne quoted Wiener 1981, pp. 41-42.
9. Idem, p. 108 and p. 97.
10. Marquand 1988.
11. Ween 1986, p. 7.
12. *The Economist*, (1987), pp. 31-32.
13. *The Art Journal*, (1851), May, p. 180.
14. *The Art Journal*, (1851), March, p. 104.
15. *The Art Journal*, (1851), April, p. 129.
16. Idem.
17. quoted Thompson 1977, p. 34. In his book *The Wealth of Nations* Adam Smith described a pin factory where the making of one pin required eighteen separate stages. Lucie-Smith 1981.
18. The book *Hard Times* by Dickens appeared in 1854.
19. quoted Thompson 1977, p. 31.
20. quoted Naylor 1971, p. 110/note 50.
21. Bayley 1979, p. 20. See also his article 'The Guilty Man', *Blueprint*, (1986), 28, pp. 30-31, in which he says: 'Most importantly, he [Morris] didn't want his life of ease and privilege spoiled, so he said he thought modern industry was a bad thing and suggested we revive the Middle Ages.' (p. 30) In this article he describes Morris as 'a genuine Gothic horror' (p. 30).
22. quoted Naylor 1971, p. 110/note 50.
23. quoted Thompson 1977, p. 654.
24. Thompson 1977.
25. See also chapter six in which I will return to the social values at greater length.
26. Wiener 1981.
27. Ashbee 1908, p. 11.
28. Newman 1975.
29. Macfarlane 1987.
30. Russell 1968, p. 129.
31. Arnstein 1973, p. 237.
32. Heyck 1982, p. 82.
33. quoted Heyck 1982, p. 100/note 54.
34. Melhuish 1988, p. 10.
35. Idem.
36. 'Broader skills of engineers are lacking', *Design*, (1983), April, p. 7.
37. 'Backward attitudes to new technology and design in Britain', *Design*, (1983), Sept., p. 5.
38. 'The UK leads in ignorance of technology', *Design*, (1986), Jan., p. 7.

39. Dixon 1987.
40. Palmer 1988.
41. Kenneth Grange in a conversation with the author 20/11/1988.

Chapter three: The Workshop of the World

1. Klemm 1983.
2. Palmer/Colton 1971.
3. Briggs 1983.
4. See also Marquand 1988.
5. Klemm 1983.
6. Hamilton 1980.
7. quoted cat. *Christopher Dresser 1834-1904*, London, (Camden Arts Centre), 1979, p. 11.
8. Naylor 1971, p. 16.
9. Hogben 1983, p. x. in cat. *British Art and Design*.
10. See Stewart 1987.
11. Landes 1965 and 1969.
12. Stone 1986, p. 18.
13. Payne 1974.
14. quoted Payne 1974, p. 107/note 134.
15. See also Briggs 1983.
16. quoted Payne 1974, p. 56.
17. Landes 1956, p. 564.
18. See also Macfarlane 1978 and 1987.
19. Marquand 1988 and Briggs 1983.
20. Van der Mark 1988.
21. Barnett 1986.
22. Stewart, M. 1987.
23. Marquand 1988, p. 144.
24. Sampson 1982.
25. Idem.
26. Artis 1986.
27. James Dyson in conversation with the author 19/11/1987.
28. quoted from a speech by Mrs. Thatcher in *Axis*, (1988), summer, p. 5.
29. McAlhone 1987, p. 10.
30. quoted McAlhone 1985, part 3, p. 19.

Chapter four: Design as a Commodity

1. In Sparke 1986, p. 60.
2. McAlhone 1987.
3. Idem, p. 19.
4. The first was AID in 1980.
5. From an undated brochure of Fitch & Co., probably 1988, p. 19.
6. McAlhone 1987.
7. Rune Gustafson in conversation with the author 18/11/1987.
8. Bruce Archer 1954, p. 13.
9. quoted Editorial of *Design*, (1957), 100, p. 23.
10. Hughes-Stanton 1966, p. 36.
11. Sparke 1986.
12. quoted MacCarthy 1982, p. 46/note 25.
13. 'Room for Consultants', *Design*, (1959), 122, p. 33.
14. Bruce Archer 1960, p. 65.
15. Bendixton 1963, p. 32.
16. In Sparke 1986, p. 63.
17. Hill a.o. 1976, p. 32.
18. Invisible exports are the export of intellectual capital.
19. Hill a.o. 1976, p. 28.
20. Idem, p. 34.
21. quoted Baynes 1983, p. 39.
22. Baynes 1983 and McAlhone 1987.
23. *Axis*, (1988), summer.
24. quoted Baynes 1983, p. 40.
25. cat. *Thirties. British Art and Design before the War*, London (Hayward Gallery), 1980 and Sparke 1986.
26. Kinross 1988, p. 30.
27. Idem.
28. McAlhone 1987. Takeovers as a phenomenon have an economic basis. For many companies they mean the possibility of expanding.
29. 'British Advertising', *The Economist*, (1988), 7568, pp. 25-28, p. 25.
30. Brian Boylan in conversation with the author 14/9/1988.

Chapter five: A Nation of Shopkeepers

1. *The Economist*, 5 December 1987, p. 20.
2. Dent Coad 1988.
3. cat. *1966 and all that*, London (Whitworth Art Gallery), 1986.
4. Philips 1984.
5. Its Swedish rival, Ikea, was to open its first British branch as late as 1987.
6. This is meant in a general sense – in terms of the concept rather than the actual goods. With Habitat it was being fashionable that came first, next to which it sold basic household articles imported from France. This does nothing to diminish the fact that the shop had tremendous status appeal and was considered 'in'.
7. Visick 1975 and Linklater 1979.
8. Baynes 1966.
9. quoted Baynes 1966, p. 21.
10. cat. *1966 and all that*, London (Whitworth Art Gallery), 1986, p. 55/note 6.
11. Visick 1977.
12. Freedman 1986.
13. *Working by Design*, report of the Design Management Conference 1987, published by the Chartered Society of Designers, London, p. 3.
14. Brian Johnson in a conversation with the author 17/11/1987.
15. quoted Miller 1984, p. 13.
16. Idem.
17. Abrams 1985.
18. Report *British Lifestyles*, published in 1987 by Mintel Publications and quoted in *Design*, (1988), 472, pp. 31-33.
19. Idem.
20. Rune Gustafson in a conversation with the author 18/11/1987.
21. Veblen 1899.
22. Report *British Lifestyles*, published in 1987 by Mintel Publications and quoted in *Design*, (1988), 472, pp. 31-33.
23. Idem.
24. quoted Angel 1985, p. 25.
25. Dent Coad 1988 ('Beyond Next').
26. Brian Johnson in a conversation with the author 17/11/1987.
27. From an undated brochure of Satherley Design Associates, probably 1987.
28. From an undated brochure of PA Design, probably 1988, p. 1.
29. Whitley 1987, p. 125.
30. Kinross 1988, p. 36.
31. See also Haug 1971.
32. In Thackara 1988, p. 97.
33. quoted Whitely 1987, pp. 95-96/note 16.

Chapter six: Social Values

1. In Hamilton 1985, p. 21.
2. Stevens/Rose 1976.
3. Mike Dempsey in a conversation with the author 26/10/1988.
4. Hamilton 1985, p. 87.
5. Paul Moss in a conversation with the author 1/11/1988.
6. Visick/Fielding 1979.
7. quoted Cooper 1988, p. 17.
8. In Hamilton 1985.
9. quoted Hamilton 1985, p. 87/note 22.
10. In Hamilton 1985, p. 20.
11. In Hamilton 1985, p. 15.
12. This is most apparent to me as a Dutch writer when making a comparison with my own country, where design in the public sector is highly developed. A greater openness in the administrative machinery, more tolerance, individual champions of art and design, and close contact between art and officialdom form a stark contrast with the situation in Great Britain.
13. Dormer 1987 ('a vote for design'), p. 24.
14. quoted Pevsner 1986, p. 39/note 17.
15. quoted Naylor 1971, p. 28.
16. Marx in *Das Kapital* (1938), quoted Thompson 1977, pp. 38-39.
17. The term Arts and Crafts was first used by T.J. Cobden-Sanderson in 1887 at a meeting of what would be known the following year as the Arts and Crafts Exhibition Society. Arts and Crafts is often spoken of as a movement, probably because its 'members' shared similar ideas on design, and had contact with one another through guilds, schools, and suchlike. Abroad, too, these British developments were considered to be a school. In fact it was not a close-knit group.
18. quoted cat. *William Morris Today*, London, (ICA), 1984, p. 44/note 4.
19. Criticism of another sort may be levelled at his directorship of a copper mine, which is how he earned his living. Ironically enough, this was the only way to keep Morris & Co going. Besides, he held this function between 1871 and 1876, whereas he became actively involved in politics only in 1877.
As employer at Merton Abbey he paid his workmen better than was the case elsewhere, and in the form of a fixed wage rather than for each piece. The working conditions were congenial in all other aspects, too.
20. quoted cat. *William Morris Today*, London (ICA), 1984, p. 134.
21. Thompson 1977, p. 721.
22. Crawford 1985, p. 421
23. A. Clutton Brock, 'A modern creed of work', reprinted in Bayley 1979, pp. 29-31, p. 29 and p. 30.
24. quoted Whitely 1987, p. 53/note 27.
25. Banham 1955, p. 25.
26. Hamilton 1960.
27. quoted Editorial of *Design*, (1965), 201, p. 25.
28. Black 1975, p. 45.
29. Christopher Frayling mentions in his book on the RCA a sit-in of film students that lasted one month but didn't lead to any results. Also he says: 'The RCA had somehow escaped the upheavals of '68 and after, except for one or two isolated incidents.' Frayling 1987, p. 158.
30. quoted Hamilton 1985, p. 9/note 9.
31. Cornford 1968, p. 46.
32. R. Banham, 'Household Godjets', reprinted in Barker 1977, p. 168.
33. Thackara 1986, p. 11.
34. In Thackara 1988, p. 129.

Chapter seven: A Passion for Utility

1. quoted Pevsner 1986, p. 202/note 12.
2. quoted Ferrey 1978, p. 314.
3. quoted Crawford 1985, p. 50/note 30.
4. quoted Naylor 1971, p. 19.
5. quoted Lucie-Smith 1981, p. 210.
6. quoted MacCarthy 1982, p. 12/note 4.
7. quoted Braidwood 1986, p. 56.
8. Dormer 1985 ('The benefits of craft . . .') p. 46.
9. 'Wanderings in the Crystal Palace, no. III', *The Art Journal*, (1851), July, pp. 230-235, p. 230.
10. quoted Naylor 1971, p. 115/note 7 en p. 169/note 11.
11. quoted Naylor 1971, p. 115/note 8.
12. quoted Brandon-Jones 1978, p. 12.
13. Carrington 1976, p. 28.
14. quoted Hamilton 1980, p. 10.
15. quoted Newman 1975, p. 10.
16. Idem, p. 27.
17. cat. *Thirties. British Art and Design before the War*, London (Hayward Gallery), 1980.
18. quoted Bayley 1983, p. 25.
19. Naylor 1971, p. 165. Incidentally the DIA was not founded in 1914 but in 1915.

20. quoted Crawford 1985, p. 419/note 91.
21. quoted Benton 1975, p. 191.
22. quoted Benton 1975, p. 193.
23. quoted Newman 1975, p. 17/note 1.
24. Read 1934 and 1935, p. 50.
25. cat. *Thirties. British Art and Design before the War*, London (Hayward Gallery), 1980.
26. quoted Brandon-Jones 1978, p. 19.
27. Newman 1975.
28. *Design*, (1949), 1, pp. 2-6, p. 2.
29. 'Pointers', *Design*, (1961), 146, p. 25.
30. Hughes-Stanton 1968, p. 42.
31. Woudhuysen/Sudjic 1985, p. 29.

Chapter eight: Artist-Craftsmen en Designer-Makers

1. This is what they said in the fifties, sixties and seventies as well, so it is not so much new, but rather different this time.
2. Pilz 1974.
3. Potter 1980.
4. The *Oxford Companion to Art* (1970) mentions that in the Italy of Vasari's day the ability to *design* was what distinguished an artist from a craftsman.
5. The American painter George Woodham claims that a pot cannot be sculpture because in its undecorated state it offers no more than a silhouette or outline. Its individual identity is thus limited to its edges. In its decorated state it attracts the attention merely as a treated surface. See Dormer 1986 (The New Ceramics).
6. cat. *Maker Designers Today*, London (Camden Arts Centre), 1984.
7. In cat. *The Maker's Eye*, London (Crafts Council), 1987, p. 24.
8. cat. *2D3D*, Sutherland (Northern Centre for Contemporary Art), 1987.
9. Fuller 1985.
10. In cat. *The Maker's Eye*, London (Crafts Council), 1987, p. 24.
11. In cat. *British Ceramics*, Den Bosch (Kruithuis), 1985, p. 14.
12. quoted cat. *2D3D*, Sutherland (Northern Centre for Contemporary Art), 1987, p. 24.
13. cat. *The Jewellery Project*, London (Crafts Council), 1983, p. 5.
14. Frayling 1987.
15. Idem, p. 160
16. *Design*, (1975), 318, p. 17 (Editorial).
17. quoted *Blueprint*, (1987), 40, p. 14.

18. Ron Arad in a conversation with the author 1/3/1988.
19. In cat. *The New Spirit in Crafts and Design*, London (Crafts Council), 1987, p. 16.
20. In cat. *The Modern Chair*, London (ICA), 1988, p. 51.
21. In cat. *London-Amsterdam. New Art Objects from Britain and Holland*, London/Amsterdam (Crafts Council/Galerie Ra/Galerie De Witte Voet), 1988, p. 21.
22. Although this can be seen as the cultural influence of countries from the British Empire, the fact that it is happening now seems to me to be significant.
23. The reasoning of critics like Peter Dormer, who sees the craft-based product as an object of contemplation, and Peter Fuller, who foists a consolatory function onto the crafts, I find difficult to follow. With this they are still harbouring hope for the symbolic role of craftwork. The French philosopher Jean Baudrillard, on the other hand, has abandoned this hope altogether. His argument is that originally everything was derived from Nature. This man transformed and cultivated in the creation of the object through labour. This is why his relation to that object was, according to Baudrillard, a symbolic one. Moreover this relation was supported by a moral order, namely tradition. But, with the coming of the Industrial Revolution, these bonds were severed, after which those crafts-based products could give man merely the illusion of authenticity, originality, and atmosphere. Baudrillard 1968.

Chapter nine: Design from the Street

1. In Thackara 1988, p. 166.
2. Peter York in conversation with the author 14/9/1988.
3. Idem.
4. quoted McDermott 1987, p. 57.
5. Idem.
6. BBC2, 31 August 1988.
7. Idem.
8. Hawkins 1988.
9. *Blueprint*, (1985), 22, p. 5.
10. quoted McDermott 1987, p. 41.
11. Idem, p. 34.
12. Suzy Menkes in a conversation with the author 1/3/1988.
13. Idem.
14. quoted Coleridge 1988, p. 145.
15. Idem, p. 125.
16. Idem.
17. cat. *The Jewellery Project*, London (Crafts Council), 1983.
18. Malcolm Garrett in a conversation with the author 26/4/1988.

19. *i-D*, The Revolution Issue, (1988), p. 16.
20. quoted Wozencraft 1988, p. 59.
21. Idem, p. 60.
22. Idem.
23. Malcolm Garrett in a conversation with the author 26/4/1988.
24. cat. *14:24 British Youth Culture*, London (Boilerhouse), 1986. Clark 1988.
25. cat. *14:24. British Youth Culture*, London (Boilerhouse), 1986.
26. quoted McDermott 1987, p. 83.
27. cat. *14:24. British Youth Culture*, London (Boilerhouse), 1986, np.
28. Esterson 1988, p. 51.

Chapter ten: The Medium is the Message

1. Wade 1985.
2. See Bódy 1987.
3. quoted Bódy 1987, p. 7.
4. Alex McDowell in a conversation with the author 15/9/1988.
5. Blair 1988. p. 68.
6. Smith 1984; Alex McDowell in a conversation with the author 15/9/1988.
7. Idem.
8. quoted Bódy 1987, p. 204.
9. Idem, p. 209.
10. Alex McDowell in a conversation with the author 15/9/1988.
11. quoted Skelsey 1986, p. 28.
12. Idem
13. Alex McDowell in a conversation with the author 15/9/1988.
14. Peter York in a conversation with the author 14/9/1988.
15. Clark 1988.
16. York 1988.
17. cat. *Images for Sale*, London (Boilerhouse), 1983; and Clark 1988.
18. Lott 1980.
19. quoted Clark 1988, p. 283.
20. Idem, p. 46
21. cat. *Images for Sale*, London (Boilerhouse), 1983.
22. quoted *Televisual*, (1988), Sept., p. 35.
23. quoted Foster 1988, p. 25.
24. Gert Dumbar in a conversation with the author 23/8/1988.
25. Clark 1988.
26. quoted Gwyther 1988, pp. 18-19.

BIBLIOGRAPHY

Abrams, J., 'Lifestyles: what next. Forecasting Tomorrow', *Blueprint*, (1985), 20, pp. 14-15

'A Feast of Fashion', *Design*, (1985), 442, pp. 48-49

Allen, C., 'Tabling the Changes', *Crafts*, (1988), 94, pp. 39-41

Ames, W., *Prince Albert and the Victorian Taste*, London 1968

Angel, S., 'Way Ahead', *Blueprint*, (1985), 22, pp. 24-27

Anscombe, I., & Gere, Ch., *Arts and Crafts in Britain and America*, London 1978

Anscombe, I., 'Knowledge is power; the design of Christopher Dresser', *Connoisseur*, (1979), May, pp. 54-59

Anscombe, I., *Omega and After. Bloomsbury and the Decorative Arts*, London 1981.

Arnstein, W.L., 'The Survival of Victorian Aristocracy', in Jamer, F.C. (ed), *The Rich, the Well-Born and the Powerful; Elites and Upper Classes in History*, Illinois 1973

Artis, M.J., *Prest and Coppock's The UK Economy*, London 1986

'As Europe sees us', *Design*, (1964), 185, p. 27

Ashbee, C.R., *Craftsmanship in Competitive Industry*, London 1908

Auty, M., & Roddick, N., *British Cinema Now*, London 1985

Banham, R., 'Household Godjets', in Barker, R. (ed), *Arts in Society*, Glasgow 1977, pp. 164-170

Banham, R., *New Brutalism. Ethic or Aesthetic?*, London 1966

Barnett, C., *The Audit of War*, London 1986

Barrè, F., 'British Design in Paris', *Design*, (1971), 268, p. 17

Baron, S., 'A Classic Case', *Crafts*, (1988), 94, pp. 23-25

Baudrillard, J., *Le systeme des objets*, Paris 1968

Bayley, S., *In Good Shape. Style in Industrial Products 1900 to 1960*, London 1979

Bayley, S., 'The guilty man: William Morris', *Blueprint*, (1986), 28, pp. 30-31

Bayley, S., *Taste,* London 1983

Bayley, S., Garner, P., & Sudjic, D., *Twentieth Century Style and Design*, London 1986

Baynes, K. & K., 'Behind the scene', *Design*, (1966), 212, pp. 19-28

Baynes, K., *Young Blood. Britain's Design Schools Today and Tomorrow*, London 1983

Bendixton, T., 'In an age of specialists does the versatile designer make sense?', *Design*, (1963), 177, pp. 29-32

Benton, T., Benton, Ch., & Sharp, D., *Form and Function. A Source Book for the History of Architecture and Design 1890-1939*, London 1975

Best, A., 'Terminal Cases', *Design*, (1974), 312, pp. 60-65

Best, A., 'Trouble in Store', *Design*, (1972), 280, pp. 30-34

Billcliffe, R., *Mackintosh Furniture*, New York 1985

Black, M., 'Design needs Art', *Design*, (1975), 321, pp. 34-36

Black, M., 'Fitness for what purpose', *Design*, (1975), 313, pp. 42-45

Blain, D., 'Sounds in Print', *Design*, (1972), 282, pp. 42-44

Blair, I., 'The weird and wonderful world of Godley and Creme', *Pulsei*, (1988), April, pp. 66-69

Blake, A., *Misha Black*, London 1984

Blakstad, M., *The Risk Business. Industry and the Designers*, London 1979

Bódy, V., & Weibel, P. (eds), *Clip, Klapp, Bum. Von der visuellen Musik zum Musikvideo*, Köln 1987

Booth-Clibborn, E. (ed), *Design à la Minale Tattersfield. A Unique Philosophy applied to all aspects of Design*, London 1986

Braidwood, S., 'Looking Backwards from Aspen', *Design*, (1986), Sept., pp. 54-59

Brandon-Jones, J. et al., *C.F.A. Voysey: Architect and Designer 1857-1941*, London 1978

Briggs, A., *A Social History of England*, Harmondsworth 1987, (first edition 1983)

Britain 1987. An Official Handbook, London 1987 (Central Office of Information)

Britton, M., 'What a management consultant can do for a design consultant', *Design*, (1979), 361, pp. 56-59

Bruce Archer, L., 'Artist versus Engineer', *Design*, (1954), July, pp. 13-16

Bruce Archer, L., 'Consultant – but how general?', *Design*, (1960), 138, p. 65

Bruce Archer, L., 'Room for the consultants', *Design*, (1959), 122, p. 33

Buchanan, P., 'A Nostalgic Utopia, or, why the British excel at High Tech', *Items*, (1985), 15, pp. 4-11

Buchanan, R.A., *Industrial Archeology in Britain*, Harmondsworth 1972

'Caring for Craftmanship', *Design*, (1973), 293, p. 17

Carrington, N., *Industrial Design in Britain*, London 1976

Carrington, N. & Harris, M., 'The British Contribution to Industrial Art 1851-1951', *Design*, (1951), 31, pp. 20-22

cat. *2D 3D. Art and Craft made and designed for the Twentieth Century*, Sutherland (Northern Centre for Contemporary Art) 1987

cat. *14:24. British Youth Culture*, London (Boilerhouse), 1986

cat. *1966 and all that. Design and the Customer in Britain 1960-1969*, London (Whitworth Art Gallery), 1986

cat. *Architect-Designers. Pugin to Mackintosh*, London (Fine Arts Society & Haslam and Whiteway), 1981

cat. *British Art and Design 1900-1960. A Collection in the Making*, London (Victoria & Albert Museum), 1983

cat. *Christopher Dresser 1834-1904*, London (Camden Arts Centre), 1979

cat. *Christopher Dresser. Ein Viktorianischer Designer 1834-1904*, Köln (Kunstgewerbemuseum), 1981

cat. *The Crystal Palace Exhibition Illustrated Catalogue London 1851*, republication of the Art Journal special issue, New York 1970

cat. *Expo. Le livre des expositions universelles 1851-1989*, Paris (Centre Pompidou), 1983

cat. *Five Furniture Pieces*, London (British Crafts Centre), 1985

cat. *Homespun to Highspeed: A Century of British Design 1880-1980*, Sheffield (Art Gallery), 1979

cat. *Images for Sale*, London (Boilerhouse), 1983

cat. *The Jewellery Project*, London (Crafts Council), 1983

cat. *Keith Murray*, London (Victoria & Albert Museum), 1976

cat. *Kenneth Grange at the Boilerhouse. An Exhibition of British Product Design*, London (Boilerhouse), 1983

cat. *London-Amsterdam. New Art Objects from Britain and Holland*, London/Amsterdam (Crafts Council Gallery, Galerie Ra, Galerie de Witte Voet), 1988

cat. *Maker Designers Today*, London (Camden Arts Centre), 1984

cat. *The Maker's Eye*, London (Crafts Council), 1981

cat. *The Modern Chair*, London (ICA), 1988

cat. *Museum of the Moving Image*, London (MOMI), 1988

cat. *National Characteristics in Design*, London (Boilerhouse), 1985

cat. *The New Spirit in Crafts and Design*, London (Crafts Council Gallery), 1987

cat. *Taste*, London (Boilerhouse), 1983

cat. *Thirties. British Art and Design before the War*, London (Hayward

Gallery), 1980

cat. *The Way We Live Now: Designs for Interiors 1950 to the Present Day*, London (Victoria & Albert Museum), 1978

cat. *William Morris Today*, London (ICA), 1984

Clark, E., *The Want Makers*, London e.o., 1988

Coleridge, N., *The Fashion Conspiracy. A Remarkable Journey through the Empires of Fashion*, London 1988

Cooper, M., 'Management Tomorrow', *Designer*, (1988), 5, pp. 14-17

Cornford, Chr., 'Cold Rice Pudding and Revisionism', *Design*, (1968), 231, pp. 46-48

Crawford, A., *C.R. Ashbee. Architect, Designer and Romantic Socialist*, New Haven/London 1985

Crick, B., '1688 – No Thank You', *NRC-Handelsblad*, 3 June 1988

D&AD Yearbooks, 1963-1987

Dale, R., 'Clive's Early Years', *Sinclair User*, (1985), 45, pp. 78-80

Dale, R., 'ZX 80 and Beyond', *Sinclair User*, (1986), 46, pp. 86-90

Davies, N., 'Godley and Creme. Permanently Engaged', *Commercial*, (1988), 10, pp. 12-13

Dent Coad, E., 'Beyond Next: New English Traditions', *Design*, (1988), 472, pp. 38-39

Dent Coad, E., Hodges, F., & Sparke, P., a.o., *Design Source Book*, London 1986

Dent Coad, E., 'Quick, Learn Italian', *Design*, (1988), 477, pp. 28-29

Derry, T.K., & Williams, T.T., *A Short History of Technology*, Oxford 1960

DIA Yearbook, *Diamond Jubilee Edition*, London 1975

Dixon, B., 'Britten ondergraven hun Wetenschappelijke Basis', *De Volkskrant*, 5 Dec. 1987

Dodsworth, T. a.o., 'UK Industrial Prospects', *The Financial Times*, 4 Jan. 1988

Doorn, F. van, 'Racisme en Sex in Merry Old England', *Haagse Post*, (1988) 23 Jan. pp. 52-53

Dormer, P., 'The Benefits of Craft to Industry', *Design*, (1985), 436, pp. 38-43

Dormer, P., 'Dyed in the Wool', *Crafts*, (1984), 69, pp. 12-13

Dormer, P., 'Give More Power to the Designer's Elbow', *The Guardian*, 12 Sept. 1984

Dormer, P., *The New Ceramics. Trends and Traditions*, London 1986

Dormer, P., *The New Furniture. Trends and Traditions*, London 1987

Dormer, P., 'Nigel and the Others', *Blueprint*, (1985), 21, pp. 28-30

Esterson, S., 'Brody on Sign Language', *Blueprint*, (1988), 46, pp. 50-52

Esterson, S., 'Mode en Traditie. Grafische Vormgeving in Engeland', *Items*, (1985), 15, pp. 25-28

Everett, P., *You'll never be 16 again*, London 1986

Ferrey, B., *Recollections of Pugin*, London 1978. (first edition 1861)

Foster, S., 'What Makes a Great Ad by Hegarthy', *Commercials*, (1988), 10, pp. 24-25

Forum, 24, (1975), 6, special issue on William Morris

Foster, H. (ed), *Postmodern Culture*, London/Sydney 1985

Frayling, Chr., *The Royal College of Art. One Hundred and Fifty Years of Art and Design*, London 1987

Freedman, L., 'Hamnett in SW3', *Blueprint*, (1986), 32, pp. 34-37

Friebe, W., *Vom Kristallpalast zum Sonnenturm. Eine Kulturgeschichte der Weltausstellungen*, Leipzig 1983

Fuller, P., 'The Craft Revival?', *Crafts*, (1984), 69, pp. 13-15

Fuller, P., *Images of God. The Consolations of Lost Illusions*, London 1985 (first edition 1982)

Gerlagh, W.J., 'Kunst en Maatschappij. William Morris en de beginjaren van het Nederlandse Socialisme', *Intermediair*, 17, (1981) nos. 28 and 29

Gibb, J., 'Sculpture and Product Identity', *Design*, (1983), Dec., pp. 50-53

Gibbs-Smith, C.H. (ed), *The Great Exhibiton of 1851. A Commemorative Album*, London 1950

Gloag, J., *Industrial Art Explained*, London 1934

Gorb. P. (ed), *Living By Design: Pentagram Design Partnership*, London 1978

Gwyther, M., 'Design and Ad Direction', *Designer*, (1988), 3, pp. 14-17

Hamilton, N. (ed), *Design and Industry: the Effects of Industrialisation and Technical Change on Design*, London 1980

Hamilton, N. (ed), *From the Spitfire to the Microchip. Studies in the History of Design from 1945*, London 1985

Hamilton, R., 'Persuading Image', *Design*, (1960), 134, pp. 28-32

Hare, A., 'The Glory of the Garden', *Crafts*, (1984), 70, p. 15

Harrison, C., *English Art and Modernism 1900-1939*, London/ Bloomington 1981

Harrod, T., 'The Pot as Product', *Crafts*, (1988), 94, pp. 14-15

Haug, W.F., *Kritik der Warenästhetik*, Frankfurt am Main 1971

Hawkins, H., 'The Quality Gap', *Design*, (1986), 445, pp. 20-22

Heller, R., 'The Naked Entrepreneur', *Design*, (1977), 342, pp. 44-49

Henrion, F.H.K., 'What Henrion says about what Olins says', *Design*, (1978), 360, pp. 44-47

Heyck, T.W., *The Transformation of Intellectual Life in Victorian England*, London/Sydney 1982

Hill, P., 'The damp squib of invention follow-through', *Design*, (1976), pp. 40-41

Hill, P., 'International Movement', *Design*, (1976), 330, pp. 28-31

Hill, P., Visick, J., & Cooper, J. a.o., 'Eye Witness Account', *Design*, (1976), 330, pp. 32-39

Hollister, J. & Theaker, A. (eds), *The Best of British Illustration and Photography*, Geneva 1987

Hughes-Stanton, C., 'How consultant designers work', *Design*, (1966), 214, pp. 36-43

Hughes-Stanton, C., 'What comes after Carnaby Street?', *Design*, (1968), 230, pp. 42-43

Huygen, F., 'The Britishness of British Design. Een interview met Floris van den Broecke', *Items*, (1985), 15, pp. 21-25

Jay, M., 'Environmental Design', *Design*, (1967), 218, pp. 44-49

Jencks, Ch., *Modern Movements in Architecture*, Harmondsworth 1977 (first edition 1973)

Jippes, H., 'Britse Staalindustrie verloor 150.000 arbeiders', *NRC-Handelsblad*, 4 Dec. 1987

Jippes, H., 'De rode Gloed is verdwenen, het Wasgoed is gebleven', *NRC-Handelsblad*, 23 Dec. 1987

Joustra, W., 'Je schiet Sinterklaas ook niet overhoop, *De Volkskrant* 27 Feb. 1988

Joustra, W., 'Rechtse Britse pers valt over linkse Films', *De Volkskrant*, 29 Jan. 1988

Kinross, R., 'From Commercial Art to Plain Commercial', *Blueprint*, (1988), 46, pp. 29-36

Klemm, F., *Geschichte der Technik. Der Mensch und seine Erfindungen im Bereich des Abendlandes*, Hamburg 1983

Klingender, F.D., *Art and the Industrial Revolution*, St. Albans 1975 (first edition 1947)

Kluge, J. (ed), *BM Stilkunde. Geschichte des Möbels*, Stuttgart 1986

Landes, D.S., 'Technological change and development in Western Europe 1750-1914', *The Cambridge Economic History of Europe, VI, The Industrial Revolutions and After*, part 1: ed. H.J. Habakkuk and M. Postan, Cambridge 1965.

Landes, D.S., *The Unbound Prometheus. Technological Change and Development in Western Europe*, Cambridge 1969

Law, H., 'Is this the train of the age?', *Design*, (1980), Aug., p. 61

Lehman, K., 'What Germany wants from British products', *Design*, (1978), 357, pp. 52-55

Levey, M., *Painting at Court*, New York 1971

Linklater, R., 'Has Burton found the Style for its Retail Comeback?', *Design*, (1979), 361, pp. 36-41

Lopes Cardozo, A., 'David Kindersley, een Engelse Lettergek', *Items*, (1985), 15, pp. 16-20

Lorenz, Chr., 'Design in British Industry', *The Financial Times*, Feb. 27 1985

Lott, J., 'Making for the Mills', *Design*, (1984) Nov. pp. 54-55

Lott, J., 'US cash vs UK dash', *Design*, (1980), 383, pp. 52-55

Lucie-Smith, E., *The Story of Craft. The Craftsman's Role in Society*, Oxford 1981

MacCarthy, F., *A History of British Design 1830-1970*, London 1979

MacCarthy, F., *British Design since 1880. A Visual History*, London 1982

Macfarlane, A., *The Culture of Capitalism*, Oxford 1987

Macfarlane, A., *The Origins of English Individualism*, Oxford 1978

Mark, D.F.W., van der, *Het Verenigd Koninkrijk. Regionaal beleid. Economische politiek. Economie*, Amsterdam 1988

Marquand, D., *The Unprincipled Society. New Demands and Old Politics*,

London 1988

McAlhone, B., *British Design Consultancy. Anatomy of a Billion Pound Business*, London 1987

McAlhone, B. (ed), *Directors on Design. A report on the 1985 SIAD Design Management Seminar on what PA Technology, Logica and British Telecom do about design*, London 1985

McAlhone, B. (ed), *Directors on Design. A report on the 1985 SIAD Design Management Seminar on how Jaguar, Austin Rover and Ford handle their design today*, London 1985

McDermott, C., *Street Style. British Design in the 80s*, London 1987

McQuiston, L., & Kitts, B., *Graphic Design Bronnenboek*, Veenendaal 1988

Melhuish, C., 'Building Bridges', *Designer*, (1988), 5, pp. 10-12

Miller, R., 'A Century of Sainsbury's', *Design*, (1969), 243, pp. 65-68

Miller, S., 'Joseph. Where fashion meets design', *Blueprint*, (1984), 8, pp. 12-13

Morris, W., *Kunst en Maatschappij. Lezingen*, Amsterdam 1903

Myerson, J., 'Art on the Sleeve', *Design*, (1984), Nov., p. 52

Myerson, J., 'Form follows Rhythm', *Design*, (1984), Nov., pp. 46-47

Nairn, T., *The Enchanted Glass: Britain and its Monarchy*, London 1988

Naylor, G., *The Arts and Crafts Movement. A Study of its Sources, Ideals and Influence on Design Theory*, London 1971

Newman, G., *A Survey of Design in Britain 1915-1939*, Milton Keynes 1975

'New Report on Design Strategy', *Design*, (1985), 434, p. 5

Olins, W., 'Englishness as Identity', *Blueprint*, (1986), 28, p. 28

Olins, W., *The Wolff Olins Guide to Corporate Identity*, London 1984

Osborn, S., 'Record Sleeve Revival', *Design*, (1980), 379, pp. 48-49

Palmer, C., 'Confessions of a Consumer', *Design*, (1988), 472, pp. 31-33

Palmer, R.R., & Colton, J., *A history of the modern world*, 1971 (first edition 1950)

Pawley, M., 'Come Back Austerity: All is Forgiven', *Blueprint*, (1986), May, pp. 18-19

Payne, P.L., *British Entrepreneurship in the Nineteenth Century*, London/ Basingstoke 1978 (first edition 1974)

'Persuading Image: a symposium', *Design*, (1960), 138, pp. 54-57

Pevsner, N., *The Englishness of English Art*, Harmondsworth 1986. (first edition 1956)

Philips, B., *Conran and the Habitat Story*, London 1984

Pilz, W., 'Zum Verhältnis von Kunst und Produktgestaltung', *Zeitschrift für Kunstpädagogik*, 2, (1974), pp. 61-72

Plowman, A., 'The Shopfitting Industry', *Design*, (1962), 167, pp. 40-44

Plum, W., *Les Expositions Universelles au 19e Siecle. Spectacles du Changement Socio-culturel*, Bonn 1977

Polan, B., 'A serious business?', *Design*, (1985), 439, pp. 40-41

Polhemus, T., & Procter, L., *Pop Style. An A-Z Guide to the World where Fashion meets Rock 'n Roll*, London 1984

Posthumus, T., 'Illustraties als pop-art', *Adformatie*, (1988), 31, p. 32

Potter, N., *What is a Designer. Things, Places, Messages*, Reading 1980

Pye, D., 'Hand Work. Its Significance Today', *Design*, (1958), 111, pp. 55-57

Ramakers, R., 'Sinclair Ontwerpen', *Items*, (1983), 10, pp. 36-38

Read, H., *Art and Industry*, London 1956. (first edition 1934)

Read, H., 'Novelism at the Royal Academy', *The Architectural Review*, (1935), Feb., pp. 45-50

Royle, E., *Modern Britain. A Social History 1750-1985*, London 1987

Rubens, G., *Lethaby*, London 1986

Russell, G., *Designer's Trade*, London 1968

Rusell, G., 'Good Design is not a Luxury', *Design*, (1949), 1, pp. 2-6

Sampson, A., *The Changing Anatomy of Britain*, London 1982

Skelsey, N., 'Creme always comes to the top with Godley', *HotShoe*, (1986), Sept., pp. 26-31

Smith, R., 'Exposed', *Record Mirror*, (1984), 23 June, pp. 12-13

Sparke, P., *Consultant Design. The History and Practice of the Designer in Industry*, London 1983

Sparke, P. (ed), *Did Britain Make It? British Design in Context 1946-1986*, London 1986

Special Issue on Design for Export, *Design*, (1968), 234

Special Railway Issue, *Design*, (1955), Sept.

Staal, G., 'Floris van den Broecke', *Items*, (1987), 24, pp. 24-27

Stevens, R., & Rose, S., 'To identify a corporate giant', *Design*, (1976), 332, pp. 42-55

Stewart, M., 'Een Schaduw hangt boven Engeland', *NRC-Handelsblad*, 30 Dec. 1987

Stewart, R., *Design and British Industry*, London 1987

Stone, L., & Fawtier-Stone, J., *An Open Elite? England 1540-1880*, Oxford/New York 1986

Sudjic, D., 'How Design grew to be Big Business', *Blueprint*, (1986), 28, pp. 15-20

Sudjic, D., 'Who Put the Art in Craft?'. *Blueprint*, (1984) Sept. pp. 16-17

Tessler, A., 'How to Succeed in Invisibles', *Design*, (1984), Dec., pp. 42-43

Thackara, J., 'Californian Air Anglo "a fiasco"', *Design*, (1985), 434, p. 5

Thackara, J. (ed), *Design after Modernism. Beyond the Object*, London 1988

Thackara, J., *New British Design*, London 1986

Thackara, J., 'Timing is All', *Design*, (1983), Oct., pp. 34-35

Thompson, E.P., *William Morris. Romantic to Revolutionary*, London 1977 (first edition 1955)

Thompson, J., 'Airline distinctions', *Design*, (1976), 327, pp. 30-35

Veblen, Th., *De Theorie van de Nietsdoende Klasse*, Amsterdam 1974. (published in 1899 as *The Theory of the Leisure Class)*

Verwey, W., 'Laatste Ronde voor het Staal', *NRC-Handelsblad*, 2 Dec. 1987

Visick, J., 'Do It by Yesterday', *Design*, (1975), 324, pp. 38-41

Visick, J., 'Why Shops Are No Fun Anymore', *Design*, (1977), 344, pp. 34-36

Visick, J., & Fielding, N., 'Can so much design ever have been managed by so few for so many', *Design*, (1979), 363, pp. 56-61

Vogels, H., 'The Englishness of some English Art', *Bijvoorbeeld*, 17 (1985), 4, pp. 28-33

Wade, G., *Film, Video and Television. Market Forces, Fragmentation and Technological Advance*, London 1985

Ween, F., 'The UK leads in ignorance of technology', *Design* (1986), Jan., p. 7

White, D., 'Ad agency or design consultant', *Design*, (1979), 361, pp. 46-49

Whitely, N., *Pop Design. Modernism to Mod*, London 1987

Wiener, M.J., *English Culture and the Decline of the Industrial Spirit 1850-1980*, Cambridge 1981

Woudhuysen, J., 'Going Down for the Third Time', *Blueprint*, (1986), 28, pp. 23-27

Woudhuysen, J., 'Head Hunting for Design', *Blueprint*, (1985), 19, pp. 20-21

Woudhuysen, J., 'Information bridges the invention/demand gap', *Design*, (1977), 343, pp. 32-35

Woudhuysen, J., 'The Last of the Inventors?', *Blueprint*, (1984), Sept., pp. 8-11

Woudhuysen, J., & Sudjic, D., 'Will Design Save the World?', *Blueprint*, (1985), 14, p. 29

Wozencraft, J., *The Graphic Language of Neville Brody*, London 1988

York, P., 'The Dream That Came True', *The Observer*, 14 Aug. 1988

York, P., 'Forget about High-Tech, Think of England', *Design*, (1983), Sept., pp. 62-63

York, P., *Modern Times*, London 1984

INDEX

2014

ILLUSTRATION ACKNOWLEDGMENTS

Addison, 68
Henry Arden, 60
Assorted Images, 146, 149
Bartle Bogle Hegarthy, 154, 168
Michael Barnett, 65
Boase Massime Pollitt, 166r.
Boymans-van Beuningen, 26, 28, 29, 44, 55, 56r., 58, 64l., 110, 111, 113, 124l., 125, 129
Brand New Ltd., 71, 74r.
Branson-Coates Architecture, 22, 134
Neil Bruce Photographic, 118
CAL Video Graphics, 169
Caroll, Dempsey & Thirkell, 94, 120l.
Cell Animation, 170
Collett, Dickenson, Pearce & Partners, 40, 164
Conran Design Group, 74l.
Anton Corbijn, 158, 159
Robin Day, 65
Design Council, 20, 21, 25, 38, 54, 59, 64r., 82, 83, 85, 95, 116r. 152
Jane Dillon, 132
Tom Dixon, 136
Ian Dobbie, 19, 24, 32, 34, 39, 47, 49, 54, 57, 61, 63, 73, 77, 79, 89, 91, 92, 104, 107,
108, 112, 115, 121, 122, 124r., 128, 137, 138, 153
Julienne Dolphin-Wilding, 135
DRU, 97
E.T. Archive, 36, 37, 42, 46, 50, 51, 105l.
Max Factor, 90l.
Fitch & Co., 86
Gailforce, 156
John Galliano, 142r.
Ken Garland, 80, 81
Tom Haartsen, 26, 28, 29, 44, 55, 56r., 58, 64l., 110, 111, 113, 124l. 125, 129, 142l.
Mannfred Hamm, 52r.
Haslam & Whiteway, 37, 43
Henrion, Ludlow & Schmidt, 99, 105r.
Ben Kelly, 150
A.F. Kersting, 116l.
Trevor Key, 30, 131, 148
Kunsthalle Tübingen, 103
Land Rover Ltd., 56l.
Danny Lane, 127r.
Leagas Delaney, 163
Lewis Moberly Design Consultants, 45, 119
Lloyd Northover, 67, 98r., 101
London Underground Ltd., 102
Alex McDowell, 145, 157